CATERING ESSENTIALS:
A guide to successful catering business.

Rodelo T. Salburo

Eric Lozarita

Alex Senara

GREEPOO INC.

ABOUT THE LEAD AUTHOR

Dr. Rodelo Torres Salburo is currently an Associate Professor in Management, College of Business and Economics at Aksum University, Axum City, Tigray Region, Federal Republic of Ethiopia. Dr. Salburo holds the degree of Doctor of Philosophy in Business Management from the University of Bohol, Tagbilaran City, a Master's degree in Business Administration and Bachelor's Degree in Hotel and Restaurant Management both from the University of the Visayas, Cebu City.

Dr. Salburo was a Banquet Service Coordinator at Marriott Hotel, Cebu City. The teaching career began when became a Hotel and Restaurant Management faculty at the University of Visayas, Cebu City, and have served for 7 years as the Dean of the School of Tourism and Hospitality Management at La Salle University, Ozamiz City and was appointed by the Commission on Higher Education (CHED) as a Regional Quality Assessor of the Hotel and Restaurant Management and Tourism Management programs of Region X. Dr. Salburo was also appointed in February 2014 by the Technical Education and Skills Development Authority (TESDA) as Competency Assessor in the National Certificates (NC II) of the Food and Beverage Services, Bartending, Housekeeping, and Front Office.

Dr. Salburo is the Founding President of the Council of Hospitality Management Deans and Heads (COHMDAH) in Region X Northern Mindanao, and also served for 2 years as the Dean of the School of Culinary, Hotel and Restaurant Services Technology at Northwestern Mindanao State College of Science and Technology, Tangub City. At present, Dr. Salburo is an ASEAN Master Trainer and Master Assessor in Hotel Housekeeping, a Hotel Business Operations Consultant of Sugbu Suites at Cebu City, and a member of the Council of Hotel and Restaurant Educators of the Philippines.

Dr. Salburo is an accomplished resource speaker of various seminars-workshops in Strategic Management, Hotel Management and Food Safety in the Philippines. These includes *Mass Training and Skills Enhancement for Grade 10 Technology and Livelihood Education (TLE) Teachers, Seminar on Table Etiquette, Seminar on Food Hygiene, Sanitation and Safety with Hazard Analysis Critical Control Point, Bar Service and Wine Appreciation and Alternative Track Career Symposia.* Further, Dr. Salburo also presented researches entitled, *Tourism in Ozamiz City* to the Council of Hospitality Management Deans and Heads, Region X and *The Marketability of the Bachelor of Science in Travel Management in La Salle University: Basis for Program Offering* at Liceo de Cagayan University as hosted by the Commission on Higher Education Region X.

Dr. Salburo is committed to the pursuit of academic excellence as well as to the success of businesses related to hospitality industry.

ACKNOWLEDGEMENT

After finishing this book, I couldn't help but wander on the stages that I have gone into. Apparently, the road to success is never an easy one. It has full of bumps, curves, and surprises. But with prayers and determination, surely, it can be achieved. The accomplishment of this book, *Catering Essentials: A guide to successful catering business,* is a manifestation of my hard work, perseverance, and dedication to the hospitality industry and to my profession. The hours that have been minutely given to every detail have paved way into the success of this book which has been painstakingly done with the guidance, support, and cooperation of the people who in one way or another have become the author's resilience:

I am indebted to **Dr. Eric Lozarita** for his exceptional competence in the creation of a software that would supplement this book. His expertise is surely commendable for all the supervision it gets. I am also thankful to **Dr. Alex Senara** for his insightful inputs which helped in the organization of the content. His brilliance is incomparable. I am extending my sincere gratitude as well to **Mr. Jezreel Faith Montes** for his time and effort in editing the manuscript. And to **Mr. Jeremy Moree** for the warm friendship and deep inspiration.

I am very privileged to have **Mr. Meseret Tsegay** for taking care of the Filipino community in Aksum University, Ethiopia. His love and care to my fellow Filipinos is an act of heroism and great benevolence. I wouldn't surpass all the tribulations that I have encountered in pursuing this academic endeavor without the presence of **My Family** who never fails to cheer me up despite the distance and physical company. And to **My Students** who are now in the different parts of the world, this success is heartfully dedicated to all of you as well.

And lastly, through HIM, I hurdled all challenges and trials. Without HIS divine love and care, I wouldn't make it this far. To my personal saviour, **JESUS CHRIST**, I thank you for always being there in times of my needs and prayers.

To God be the Glory!

PREFACE

This practical handbook presents an informative guide on starting up a catering business. It is written by a food service professional who has been in the industry for more than 10 years. The author shares knowledge and expertise in various fundamentals of creating a successful catering business. Further, the author carefully emphasizes the importance of becoming an effective, efficient, and effectual caterer by including tips, reminders, and concrete solutions on certain issues and concerns in catering.

This handbook is a valuable resource material to all aspiring caterers and even professional caterers. The guide notes are very simple and easy to follow. Important information have been highlighted for better understanding.

The handbook also has discussion questions to follow up comprehension and would further facilitate classroom interaction and learning. Generally, this handbook is for everybody who wants to have a successful catering business.

Dr. Rodelo T. Salburo
Lead Author

Axum City
Federal Republic of Ethiopia

Chapter 1

Customer Service for Catering Operations

Learning Objectives
1. Apply the qualities of a good customer service in catering operations.
2. Show how to handle customer complaints in food service effectively.
3. Discuss the importance of customer service in catering operations.
4. Actualize the need of an establishment to be service-oriented in dealing with customers.

Definition of Customer Service

Customer Service is the company's act of providing and delivering professional, helpful, and proficient assistance to the customers' needs and to those who buy or use its product and related services.

The services done to the customers are provided before, during and after purchasing and using the goods and the products. A good customer service meets the expectations of the customers and thus, provides an experience that satisfies them while an unpleasant customer service creates dissatisfaction and thus, generates complaints and grievances. It can downsize sales because customers might shift the next transaction to the closest competitor.

Catering Essentials: A guide to successful catering business

The Importance of Customer Service

Customers are the people who keep the company in business. They are there to patronize the products and services offered to them. Thus, food service establishments must be customer service oriented. This is achieved by training their employees in developing high-class customer dealings to create customer satisfaction. This satisfaction then generates loyal customers and frequent patrons.

Happy and satisfied customers will recommend your banquet and catering services to their friends, colleagues, and relatives. This then becomes your Word-of-Mouth Advertisement. According to the Nielsen Global Trust in Advertising Survey, 92% of people trust recommendations from friends, as it turns out, consumers trust word-of-mouth more than anything else. Your targeted marketed will eventually expand as new clients become your frequent customers because they have been informed on the satisfaction you have given to the previous customers. Therefore, every aspect of the banquet and catering services should focus on exceeding customers' expectations.

Good quality customer service must be primarily considered as a future investment. This could well turn into impressive turnover if favorable word-of-mouth evaluation spread far and wide.

Giving good customer service does not only aim to increase sales, but it also aims to establish a good reputation in the food industry. Eventually, with a very fine status in the industry, your catering business becomes a trusted brand-name. This would be a good driving motivation of your staff to do the best of their abilities in serving the customers excellently.

Qualities of Good Customer Service

Enticing food presentation and tasty dishes are excellent features of a food establishment, but customers do not come back anymore if they have had bad experiences with the services offered to them. It is essential that a training in developing good customer service to employees must be periodically done to help your establishment attain sales target. As the National Restaurant Association puts it, employing people who love to serve is the first step in opening a food service business that offers great customer service. After that, you train them how to serve by showing them examples of great customer service and by explaining how they can personate those examples.

These are the qualities a food service staff must emulate to be effective, proficient, and better in dealing with the customers:

1. **Politeness**: Saying *"Hello," "Good Afternoon," "Thank you very much,"* and *"How may I help you?"* to the customers shows respect and courtesy. These are practical applications of showing good manners and etiquette. And these too are essential in the food service business.

2. **Personalization**: Addressing a customer appropriately in his name is highly effective in producing loyalty. The use of *"Sir"* and *"Ma'am"* makes the customers comfortable and dignified. They like the idea that the staff of the establishment know them on a personal level.

3. **Promptness**: Customers on a food establishment are on a time table. Time is of their essence. The longer you let them wait, the worse the experience they get. Promises for the execution of catering services must be sharply on time. Delays in venue set-up and other *mise-en-place* preparations should be avoided. If there are inevitable circumstances of the delays, the customers must know. An immediate alternative must be done to compensate the customer's waiting period. The food

service workforce should come at least 30 minutes before their time-in.

4. Professionalism: Customers come in various dispositions and stance. Dealing with them vary according to their background and as a food service staff, who is well-trained to perform the job well, he is expected that he has the skill, the good judgment and the polite behavior needed in dealing with them. By showing professionalism, he must exude tolerance for difficult customers; must be tactful in words; must be careful of overtones and expressions used; and show consistent adherence to service standards. Professionalism shows that the customers are being taken care of.

5. Availability and visibility: Many customers are hesitant to actually walk into the bar or to the counter to ask for something. So, they only channel their concerns and requests through a food service staff they see around. When concerns need urgent attention and customers do not see a staff nearby, tendency is, they become irate and impatient resulting to dissatisfaction. By being visible, you make the guest feel they are having a better experience because they know that if they need something, you are available to provide assistance.

6. Being Exceptional: Customers can get good food and decent services anywhere provided that the food establishment is of good quality and service. What will set your catering apart from others is the degree to which you are willing to go beyond to be incomparable. Catering employees may employ this service by making special creations for customers such as offering them drinks to go, giving complementaries like mints after the banquet and engaging in other little practices that show your catering is beyond comparable.

Common Guest Complaints in Food service establishments

There are some customers who are hard to please. But most of the time, customers' dissatisfaction arises from actual events and situations that can be handled. To help

prepare your catering business and employees for these challenging encounters, let us take a look at some of the common sources of complaints:

1. **Product Knowledge:** Customers get easily irritated and become irate when an employee does not know specifically an answer to their questions such as the ingredients in the catering's signature dish, or prices for debut and wedding catering packages. Customers expect an immediate answers which are clear, concise, and brief. To minimize these potential complaints, employees who work directly with customers must know the following:

   a. The products and services they are selling or offering. It also includes the product's ingredients, allergens, nutrition facts, dietary concerns, pricing, etc.
   b. The appropriate authority for the customer's question or demands should the employee unable to give exact answers. It shall be asked then through the dining supervisor, chef, and other administrative staff of the establishment.

2. **Rude Food Service Staff:** A rude staff triggers complaints from the customers. However, rudeness can take many ways, which may not always be obvious to you or your employees. For instance, an aloof tone of voice, indifference, inattentiveness, or has a defensive attitude and body language can be largely annoying to few customers. To prevent these complaints, your food service staff must observe the following:

   a. Use proper communication skills in both verbal and nonverbal languages;
   b. Listen to the customers attentively by discriminating minute and important details;

Catering Essentials: A guide to successful catering business

    c. Know the key terms or the phraseology for better understanding with the customers; and

    d. Possess the right attitude, gestures, and facial expressions in dealing with customers.

3.   **Inaccessibility:** Customers who experience difficulty in contacting you through email, phone calls, and even speaking to the right person create displeasure. To avoid short-tempered customers, you need to be sure of the following:

    a. Keep your land line and website active all the time.

    b. Update and show your catering business' contact information on your website, brochures, leaflets, menus and social media sites. Indicate the following:
- Phone number
- Physical address
- Email address
- Page in the Social Networking Sites

    c. Show the hours of your operation and stick to those hours. A manager or someone with decision-making power is around throughout the business day.

4. Unsolved Problems: If the guest raises a complaint or has an issue, don't leave them in the air. Unsolved issues seldom fade away, they will likely turn up again in the form of an unpleasant online review that would create negative publicity.

To alleviate problems like this, be sure to

    a. Reply all inquiries in a timely fashion;

    b. Acknowledge that you received their complaint, concern or query;

    c. Express your plans to handle or resolve their concern; and

    d. Thank them for bringing it to your attention.

Steps in Dealing Guest Complaints

In the catering operations, everyone has to deal with an unhappy customer, may he be complacent, unsatisfied, or just merely demanding. Customers may be irritating sometimes and irrational when it comes to their requests. So, the great challenge there is

posed on the manner how you handle the situation as professional as possible. It should be handled in a way that the customers would think that you have operated the business well and orderly.

In some aspects, many customers do not bother to complain. Instead, they simply leave and avail of the food service from the competitors. Research suggests that up to 80% of those customers who left are actually satisfied with the services of the former food establishment. Apparently, customer satisfaction does not only determine the success of the food establishment. Delighting the customers in all aspect would earn the businesses loyalty from the customers.

If the food service staff has the competence in dealing complaints, it will surely turn dissatisfied customers into active and loyal patrons of your banquet and catering business. Here are some tips used in most hotels and food service establishments in handling upset customers:

1. **Listen carefully to what the guest has to say, and let them finish.**
Don't be defensive. The customer is not attacking you personally; he has a problem and is upset. Kindly repeat what you have heard to show that you indeed have listened to his concerns.

2.   Ask questions in a caring and concerned manner.

Ask politely. The more information you get from the customer, the better you understand his viewpoints. Ask him first a few questions before jumping in to your conclusions.

3.   Put yourself in their shoes.

As a trained food service staff, your goal is to solve the problem, not argue. The customer needs to feel like you are on his side and that you understand his situation.

4.   Apologize without blaming.

When a customer senses that you are sincerely sorry, it usually neutralizes him. Do not blame another person or department for an inconvenience caused instead, just say that you are sorry about it.

5.   Ask the guest, *"What would be an acceptable solution to you?"*

Whether or not the customer knows what a good solution would be, it is best to propose one or more solutions to soothe his agitation. Become a partner with the customer in solving the problem.

6.   Solve the problem quickly!

Research shows that customers prefer that the person they are speaking with help them solve the problems because they feel ease and comfort towards him. When complaints are brought to the higher-ups in the organization, they become more expensive to handle and they only add to the guest's disappointment.

Customer complaints are present in all sorts of food service business operations. However, by utilizing these steps and setting ample time to review on the issues, you can turn challenges into something formative then eventually be of used to it should further similar concerns happen again.

When Quality Customer Service is not enough

Mistakes are sometimes unavoidable. Unfortunately, some mistakes have consequences that a free meal or discount could not fix the problem.

Example: A customer didn't know a dish was prepared with oyster sauce and this has resulted him to a serious medical condition

A waiter loses balance and accidentally dropped the very hot sizzling steak plate on the customer

In situations like this, business insurance can be your last resort when these unforeseen events happen and your catering is sued for damages. Sufficient insurance coverage can protect your finances and help you cover the high cost of attorney's fees and court-ordered compensatory damages.

==

Key terms

1. Phraseology

2. Allergens

3. Delight

4. Physical address

5. Formative

6. Online review

7. Enticing

8. Higher-ups

==

Discussion Questions

1. What are the qualities of a good customer service?

2. What are the common guest complaints in food service business?

3. How do you show these qualities in serving the customers?

4. How do you handle guest complaints?

5. How important is customer service in catering operations?

6. Why does an establishment need to be service-oriented in dealing with customers?

==

References

Customer Service. (2015). The food industry: How to provide superior customer service. Available at http://www.wranx.com/the-food-industry-how-to-provide-superior-customer-service

Insureon Press Releases. (2016). Food services; resources grow customers. Available at http://www.insureon.com/press-releases/archive/press_release.aspx

Mckinney, P. (2015). Customer service definition. Available at http://study.com/academy/lesson/what-is-customer-service-definition-types-role-in-marketing

Miranda, M. (2016). What are examples of good service in the restaurant industry? Available at http://smallbusiness.chron.com/examples-good-service-restaurant-industry-38058.html

Ridler, B. (2016). Six Steps in Dealing Customer Complaints. Available at https://www.eonetwork.org/octane-magazine/special-features/sixstepstodealingwithcustomercomplaints

Chapter 2

Menu Planning and Pricing

Learning Objectives

1. Describe the process and rules in developing a menu.
2. Explain the purpose of a menu in catering services.
3. Enumerate the types of meal usually served in catering.
4. Analyze the importance of cost pricing methods.
5. Calculate menu price based on standards.

Developing a Menu

Menu is considered the heart of a restaurant or any other food establishment. Without its items, a food establishment is more than nothing than an empty shell. Developing a menu will substantiate the establishment's brand concept and satisfy the customers' expectations. It is one of the most important jobs a chef, a restaurateur, or a catering operator will do. Menu is the primary method of communicating to customers. Through it, the customers feel the statement the food establishment is trying to convey. Menu is a list of food and beverage for sale in a food service establishment. It dictates and controls the ingredients to be purchased, kitchen tools and equipment to be used, and the dishes to be prepared by the food service staff.

Rules to Consider in Developing Menu for Catering

1. Competition

Competition in the food industry is very tough. Setting you apart from all others is determined by how you are well aware and knowledgeable of your competitors' competency – the dishes they specialized, the events they mostly cater, and the services, facilities, and prices they offer. Identifying these factors helps you to decide to offer something creative, different, and peculiar to the customers. You must be carefully competitive on offering the prices, setting the quality of food, presenting the facilities and giving off customer service.

2. Location

You need to consider the site in which your business will operate and type of customers you are going to entice. These two things will determine the menu you are going to prepare and the services you are going to give. Customer's purchasing power will also influence the price of your menu and catering packages.

If you are in an area that grows or produces specialty foods, such as cultured crabs and shrimps, include it in the ingredients for extra menu appeal.

3. Religion

Another to be considered in developing a menu is the religious affiliation of your customers. This will strongly influence the menu items that you will include. *Example: If the bulk of your customers are Muslims, halal foods should be considered. Also, the Orthodox community do not eat pork.* So, a careful selection of ingredients other than meat is one thing that menu developer should take a look at.

4. Nutritional Adequacy and Dietary Requirements

People nowadays are very conscious on the nutrients of the food they are eating. They are careful on the label of packed and bottled food that shows nutritional facts. Ensuring a nutritionally well-balanced menu, you need also to consider in the creation of your menu the dietary requirements of the different age groups. *Example: You are catering the party event of the elderly. Do not forget to include options for the vegans.*

5. Food allergies

There are customers who are very cautious in the food they eat because of some serious medical conditions which are triggered by allergies. Usually the common allergies are found on chicken, shellfish, fish, milk, eggs, and nuts. To ensure safety among customers, it is best advised to provide a short description of ingredients in each food item listed on the menu. The food service staff as well should have a good knowledge on the products they are serving, so they can provide enough information to the guests and immediately seek for possible alternatives of the ingredients.

6. Space and equipment in the kitchen

There should be enough work space area and complete set of cooking tools and equipment to cater large quantity of food production or cater specialized menu items. Do not include dishes on the menu that the kitchen cannot comfortably produce; if not, the food service and quality will be at stake.

7. Chef's specialization

The chef's specialization is one thing that you should also prepare carefully. If you would like to operate a catering that specializes Chinese foods or Western Cuisine, then you need to look for a chef who has a specialized skill in preparing such dishes. Just because certain food items are fashionable, do not adopt a style in your menu, without fully researching and understanding it. Doing so, you are risking the reputation of your food service establishment.

8. Costs

The cost of operating the menu is an important consideration. Be aware of your food costs at all times and stay within your budget. Standardized the recipes, oversee the whereabouts of your kitchen staff, ask them to submit ingredient consumption report, and cross check with the quantified recipes. Using available computer programs will help you analyze menu cost swiftly and regularly. *(Food costing and recipe scale-up will be discussed in Chapter 4)*

9. Supplies

Include only the dishes on the menu which ingredients are readily available in large quantities in the supermarket, from a trusted supplier, or nearby stores. This would avoid disappointments from the loyal customers.

10.   Include Seasonal Fresh Items

The time of a year plays a large factor in determining food and beverage you are capable of serving. Special holidays create good vibes to customers when it comes to dining out to their favorite food establishment. This is a good reason to make a little twist when developing menu for catering special events. You can as well take into consideration which food items are in season (*fruits, vegetables and shellfish*) so as to be integrated on the menu.

11.   Food Presentation

As the famous adage says it, *"we eat with our eyes and nose before actually tasting the dish"*. This means that before tasting the food, we actually consider how does the food look like or smell like. Whether the food is served plated, in a buffet, or catered, the meal should be visually interesting, appetizingly fragrant and mouth-watering.

Linens and decorations *(table napkins, table cloths, flower centerpieces and candelabras)* should relate to theme of the meal. If it does not look and smell good, surely, customers will be disappointed. The overall presentation of food should entice the customers to eat it.

Standardized Recipe

Standardize all the recipes of the menu you have in your catering so that whoever will be assigned as cook in the kitchen, they are well guided by the standard measurements. There is only one version of preparation in each of the recipe.

The following are the specific reasons that would convince you why there is a need of standardizing your recipes.

1.   It will guard your food expense from exceeding the cost margin if standard measurements are followed.

2.   It maintains consistency of taste, texture and number of portions.

3.   It easily monitors supply consumptions.

4.   It prevents stealing incidents of food supplies and ingredients.

Types of Meals

Breakfast

Basically breakfast are classified into three:

1.   Filipino Breakfast: a typical Filipino breakfast consist of egg *(sunny side-up, scramble, omelet or hard boiled),* fried or plain rice, a choice longanisa, tocino, beef tapa or dried salted fish.

Beverage: *Coffee, tea or juice*

2.   American Breakfast: consist of bacon, sausage, scrambled eggs, hash-brown potato and toast or pancakes with syrup & blueberries, breakfast cereal with fresh milk.

Beverage: *Coffee, tea or juice*

3.   Continental Breakfast: is also known as light breakfast *(not heavy).*

It consists of sliced bread with butter/jam/honey, cheese, meat, croissants, pastries and rolls.

Beverage: *Coffee, tea or juice*

Brunch

Brunch combines the breakfast and the lunch which is usually eaten late in the morning or before noontime. It originated in England in the late 19th century and enjoyed by many people in the United States in 1930s.

Here are some rules when planning a Brunch:

1. Eggs are prepared in various styles.
2. More than two but not many kinds of fruits, vegetables and juices.
3. Ample amount of hot chocolate drink, coffee, and tea.
4. Sparkling wine is a famous brunch drink.
5. Meat dishes: bacon, ham, sausage, pork or lamb chops, crab, fish, chicken, and cheese.
6. Rice, pancakes, bread, crepes, toasts and pastries.

Lunch/ Dinner

Lunch is a noon time meal that can be buffet style or sit-down *(Plated or Russian service)*. In most food service establishments, serving of lunch starts at 11:30 in the morning and the dining areas closes at 2:00 in the afternoon. For dinner, it starts at 5:00 in the afternoon and usually closes at 11:00 in the evening. In catering service, the start of serving meal depends on the organizer or client's preference.

The sit-down meal follows the standard meal sequence: Bread & Butter, Appetizer, Soup, Salad, Side dish, Main dish and Dessert.

Lunch/ Dinner Menu Sample

Appetizer	Crispy Cheese Sticks
Soup	Bird's nest with quail eggs
Salad	Chef's Green Salad
Side Dish *(white meat)*	Chicken Relleno
Main Dish *(red meat: pork or beef)*	Beef with onions

Cereal/Grain	Garlic Fried Rice
	Mashed Potatoes
Dessert	Mango Moose
	Chocolate Moist Cake
Beverage	Soft drinks
	Four Seasons Juice
	Hot Coffee or Tea

Cocktail

Other catering clients would prefer the cocktail party which is the stand-up affairs. Cocktail buffet table (*with display of finger foods/ bite size pieces: Hors d' oeuvre is a small tidbit*) should be set up in the venue. A mobile/movable bar can be set up to add class in the venue. Bartenders will mix drinks both mocktail and cocktail.

Mocktail is a mixed drink with no alcoholic beverage added, while cocktail contains alcohol. Cocktail drink can be Vodka based, Rum based or Tequila based. Flairtending exhibition of your bartender is a plus factor in your cocktail catering service.

Movable Bar/ Portable Bar for Cocktail Parties

Menu Pricing Techniques

As mentioned in the chapter 1, pricing should be bench-marked on the purchasing power of your customer or the socioeconomic status of the area where you operate and the prevailing prices of your competitors. The price of the menu should be appealing to customers.

The Factor Pricing Method and All Cost Pricing Method are widely used in food service establishments.

Factor Pricing Method

The factor method is also know as mark-up system. The Raw Food Cost is multiplied by a pricing factor or divide by the desired food cost percentage to arrive at the selling price.

selling price = RFC X Factor

where

$$\text{Factor} = \frac{100}{\text{desired food cost percentage}}$$

or

$$\text{selling price} = \frac{\text{RFC}}{\text{desired food cost percentage}}$$

Standardization of recipe with corresponding ingredient cost should be established for consistency reasons and for easy tracking of the production cost. *(food costing will be discussed in chapter 4)* The factor is obtained by dividing the desired food cost into 100. The desired food cost in most food service establishments ranges from 24 to 34 percent. Suppose we use the 30 percent desired food cost. The factor will be

$$\frac{100}{30} = 3.33 \text{ (factor)}$$

The RFC is then multiplied by 3.33 to obtain the selling price. If the RFC on a menu item is P50.00, the selling price will be

P50.00 X 3.33 = P166.50 or P166.00 will appear as price in your menu

You can also get the selling price by dividing the RFC by the desired food cost percentage

P50.00

All Cost Pricing Method

This method takes into account all the cost involved in running the business. In addition, the percentage of profit desired from each menu item is added before establishing a selling price.

RAW FOOD COST (ingredient cost), and the two LABOR COSTS, preparation cost (chef/cook salary) and service cost (waiter's salary).

Example:

Divide the service cost by the number of guests served to get the service cost per guest, you may use the productivity ratio

Buffet (self service)	*1 waiter for every 30 guests*
Plated service	*waiter for every 15 guests*
Russian service	*1 waiter for every 10 guests*

You also have to consider the capacity of your waiters, the new ones are a bit slower in giving service compared to the seasoned waiters. Adjustments can be made in giving workload. The pay varies on work experience and you can arrange part-time waiters or on-call basis for off-premise catering.

These costs would then be added to the RFC to obtain the total cost for dish. The desired profit percentage is subtracted from 100 and divided into the total cost to arrive at the selling price.

Suppose the total cost of dish is P50.00 and the management wants 20 percent profit.

$$\text{selling price} = (100-20)\% \quad \frac{50}{} = 80 \text{ or } 0.80$$

$$\frac{50}{0.80}$$

$$= P\ 62.50$$

Handling Menu Price Increases

There is both a practical and a psychological side in handling price increases. From the practical side, as cost increases, profits decreases. Increase of cost could come from things like an increase in the minimum wage, higher or wholesale prices charged for food ingredient supplies.

Typically, an increase in costs means an increase of prices. The key is to increase prices while maintaining the number of your customers such that sales volume is maintained.

Generally speaking, for minimum negative impact, price increases should be limited to 2 to 5 percent. Prices should also be kept stable during four to six customer visits. If an increase in the prices of food supplies is announced, the time increase menu prices is when the announcement is made public rather than when the increase in prices is passed on the operator.

The reason for this is psychological, the public is aware of increased prices and, as such, is more likely to accept it at that time rather than later, when the memory of the price increase has vanished from their minds.

===

Key terms

1. Brunch
2. Buffet service
3. Plated service
4. Russian service
5. Cocktail
6. Mark-up
7. Food cost percentage
8. Off-premise catering

===

Discussion Questions

1. What is a menu?
2. What are the rules you need to consider in developing a menu?
3. In what ways do these rules help in developing a menu?
4. How do you observe a standardized recipe?
5. Why should there be a distinction among breakfast, brunch, lunch, and dinner?
6. How does the knowledge on cost pricing methods able to help the food service staff, the management, and even customers per se?
7. What importance do you see in following the standard in menu calculation?

===

Exercises

Menu Pricing

Menu item	RFC	FC %	Selling Price	Profit
Chicken lollipop	P70.00	30		
Rellenong bangus	P85.00	28		
Maja blanca	P65.00	25		
Pork asado	P90.00	30		
Custard pie	P75.00	33		

Let's try cost and sales

1. Given following information, calculate food cost percentage

a. Cost   P130; Sales P500   <u>33.33%</u>

b. Cost   P 220; Sales P600   _____

c. Cost   P1500; Sales P5500   _____

2. Calculate food cost, given the following figures for cost percentage and sales

a. FC% 30%; Sales P500   <u>P 150.00</u>

b. FC% 25%; Sales P400   _____

c. FC% 33%; Sales P700   _____

3. *Calculate Sales, given the following figures for cost percentage and cost*

a. FC% 28%; Cost P1300   <u>P 4, 642.85</u>

b. FC% 25%; Cost P1200   _____

c. FC% 33%; Cost P1600   _____

References

Christie Mill, R. (2001). Restaurant Management: Customers, Operations and Employees, USA: Prentice Hall Publishing.

Drysdale, J. A. (1998). Profitable Menu Planning. Upper Saddle River, NJ: Prentice Hall.

Eckstein, E. F. (1983). Menu Planning. Westport, CT: AVI Publishing.

Harmer, J. (2008. February). Menu Planning, *Essentially Catering Magazine*, 2. Retrieved from https://www.essentiallycatering.co.uk/issue2/menu-planning/

Hard, R. (2016). Plan a Catered Event Menu That Will Impress Your Guest. Retrieved from http://eventplanning.about.com/od/catering/tp/plancatering.htm

Jones, T. (2004). Culinary Calculations: Simplified Math for Culinary Professionals. Hoboken, NJ: John Wiley.

Labensky, S. R. (1998). Applied Math for Food Service. Upper Saddle River, NJ: Prentice Hall.

Lansing, M. (1980). Menu Planning. Michigan Dept. of Education Food and Nutrition Program School Management Services

Mackenzie, H. & Sanford, J. (1997). Menu Planning: Advanced Cuisine Knowledge. Box Hill, Vic.: Box Hill Institute of TAFE.

McCosker, K. (2013). Menu Planning. Caloundra, Qld.: 4 Ingredients.

Miller, J. E. (1976). Menu Pricing. Boston: Cahners International.

Pavesic, D. V. (1999). Restaurant Manager's Pocket Handbook: 25 Keys to Profitable Success. New York, NY: Lebhar-Friedman.

Rhodes, S. S. (1991). Effective Menu Planning for the Elderly Nutrition Program. Chicago, IL: American Dietetic Association.

The Maya Kitchen. (2004). Food service and Catering Management: A practical guide. Pasig City: Anvil Publishing House.

Visick, H. E., and Van Kleek P. E. (1973). Menu Planning: A Blueprint for Better Profits. New York: McGraw-Hill.

Zaccarelli, H. E. & Maggiore, J. (1973). Menu Planning: Food Purchasing and Management. West Lafayette, IN: Purdue U.

Chapter 3

Catering Facilities and Manpower Requirements

Learning Objectives
1. Acquaint with the basic kitchen tools and service equipment used in catering services.
2. Set up enticing buffet station to serve the customers efficiently
3. Explain the manpower requirements in catering to achieve goals in customer service.

Essential in catering services is to be equipped with kitchen tools and equipment appropriate for serving the menu. Also, food service staff must be provided with corresponding food service tools in performing table services dutifully and effectively. You might as well be needing a delivery van to transport your food, service facilities, and manpower to the site of the event of your catering services.

Kitchen Tools and Equipment

1. **Heavy duty burners** (propane burner)

   It is not appropriate to use home-based gas ranges since they cannot handle large quantity food production. Heavy duty burners should be installed in the kitchen to expedite the production process.

2.   **Cooking tools**

As mentioned in Chapter 2, your choice of menu dictates the kind of kitchen utensils that you are going to acquire. You may ask the guidance of your chef in the acquisition of kitchen tools.

Basic Cooking Tools

2.1 Hot and cold dishes cooking tools

Utensils used in preparing hot dishes (soup, hot appetizers, Side dish, Main dish) and Salads.

2.1.1 Stock pots   2.1.2 Wok   2.1.3 non-stick frying pans

   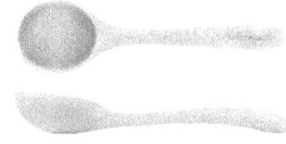   

2.1.4 Stainless ladle   2.1.5 Wooden ladle   2.1.6 Small mixing bowls

2.1.7 Stainless tong   2.1.8 Slotted spoon   2.1.9 Salad mixing bowl

Catering Essentials: A guide to successful catering business

2.1.10 Funnel   2.1.11 Colander   2.1.12 Color coded chopping boards

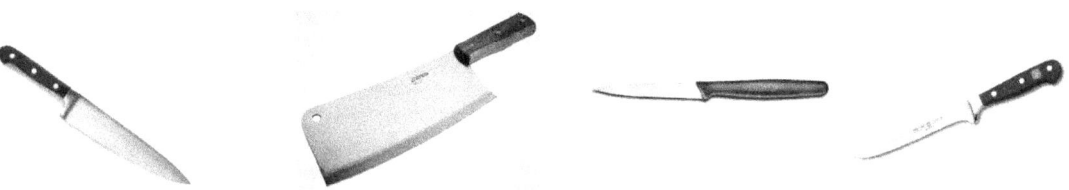

2.1.13 Chef's knife   2.1.14 Butcher's knife   2.1.15 Fruit Pairing 2.1.16 Deboning

2.1.17 Fruit carving   2.1.18 Fruit & Vegetable 2.1.19 Steamer   2.1.20 Pressure

set   peeler   Cooker

2.1.21 Weighing scales   2.1.23 Beaker   2.1.24 Food Thermometer

2.2 Bread & Pastry cooking tools and equipment

2.2.1 Oven   2.2.2 Microwave   2.2.3 Kitchen Aid

 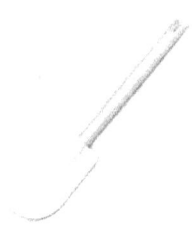 

2.2.4 Measuring cups & spoons   2.2.5 Plate & Bowl scraper   2.2.6 Mixing bowl

 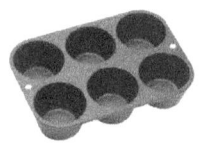 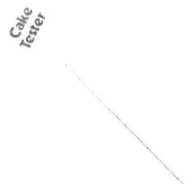

2.2.7 Baking pans   2.2.8 Muffin molder   2.2.9 Cake tester

2.2.10 Dough cutter   2.2.11 Icing bag with tips   2.2.12 Wire

whisk

Food service Tools and Equipment

It is necessary in catering that you have to invest for the complete set of service utensils and equipment. Quality food and customer service should be supported with quality utensils and equipment. Guests will be happier seeing the venue with complete set-up.

1. Silverwares/ Flatwares

1.1 Dinner knife & fork   1.2 Salad fork and knife   1.3 Fish

fork and knife

   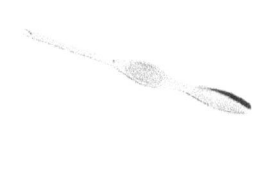

1.4 Steak knife and fork   1.5 Bread & butter knife   1.6 Lobster/ crab fork

1.7 Escargot fork & tong for snail   1.8 Cake fork   1.9 Cocktail fork

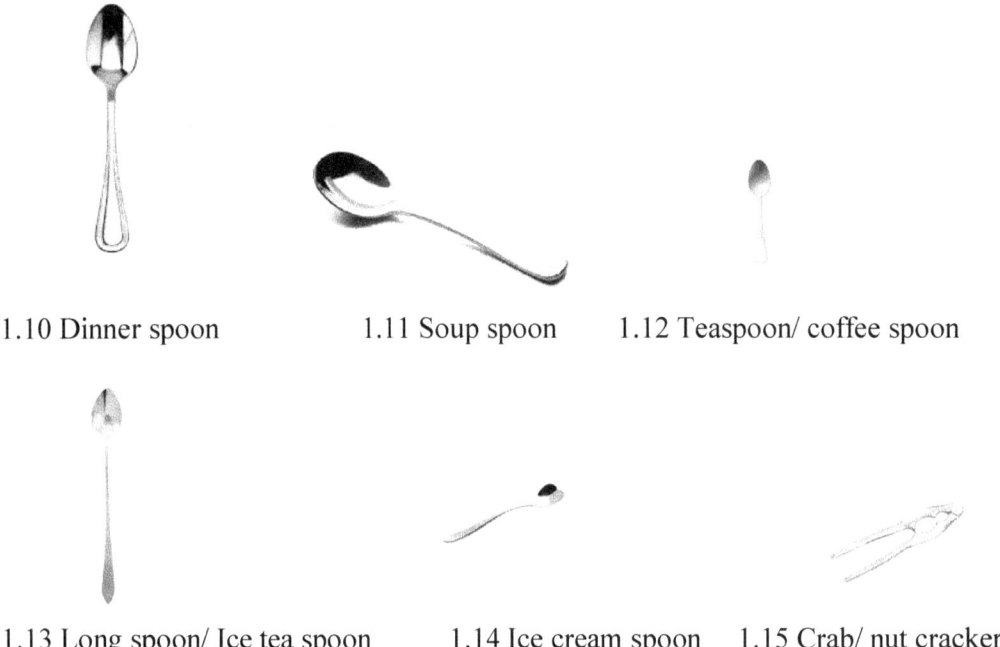

1.10 Dinner spoon   1.11 Soup spoon   1.12 Teaspoon/ coffee spoon

1.13 Long spoon/ Ice tea spoon   1.14 Ice cream spoon   1.15 Crab/ nut cracker

2. Dinnerware/ Chinaware

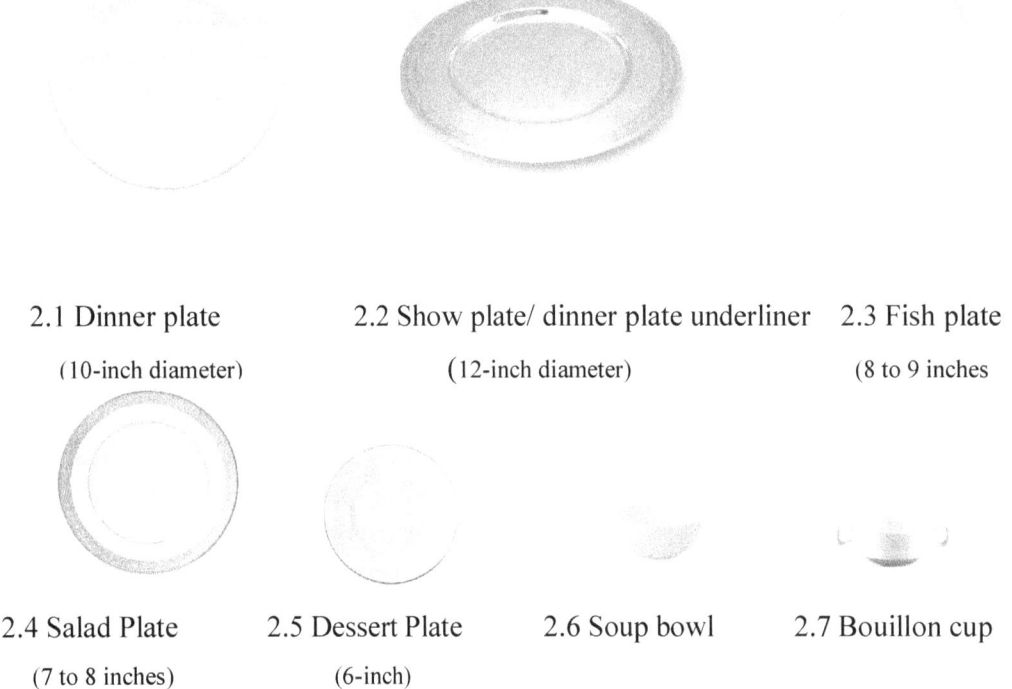

2.1 Dinner plate   2.2 Show plate/ dinner plate underliner   2.3 Fish plate

(10-inch diameter)   (12-inch diameter)   (8 to 9 inches

2.4 Salad Plate   2.5 Dessert Plate   2.6 Soup bowl   2.7 Bouillon cup

(7 to 8 inches)   (6-inch)

Catering Essentials: A guide to successful catering business

3.   **Glassware/ Beverage wares**

In handling of cocktail party events, it is necessary to be equipped with complete set of glasses in sufficient number to properly service the guests.

<u>Footed glasses</u>

3.1 Water Goblet   3.2 Poco Grande   3.3 Squal   3.4 Brandy snifter

Note: Poco grande and squal can be used in serving cocktail drinks.

<u>Stem Glasses</u>

3.5 Red & White   3.6 Champagne Tulip   3.7 Champagne flute   3.8 Champagne

wine glasses   saucer

Catering Essentials: A guide to successful catering business

3.9 Margarita glass   3.10 Cocktail glass

Tumblers

3.11 Highball   3.12 Collins   3.13 Rock glass   3.14 Beer mug

Note: highball and collins can be used in serving soft-drinks, juices, and iced tea, while the rock glass is for straight drinks like scotch on the rock.

4.   **Service Tables**

Legs of the tables should be detachable for easy storing, maximizing storage spaces for easy transport in case of off-premise catering.

4.2 Square table

(37 inches)

4.1 Round Table

75 inches in diameter (12 pax)

63 inches in diameter (10 pax)

54 inches in diameter (8pax)

Catering Essentials: A guide to successful catering business

4.3 Long table for seminars

4.4 Square cocktail table (19 inches)   4.5 Quarter table

4.5 Half-moon table

4.6 Crescent tables

Buffet Table Arrangements

In setting up buffet station, you may use various shapes of tables to create dramatic effect.

Long table with round tables at both ends

Long and two half-moon tables

3 long tables and 1 round   *long table and 1 round as centerpiece*

Ready-made double pleats skirting cloth

5. Service Trays and Tray stand

All food service trays used by waiters are rubberized to prevent the sliding of contents while transporting it to the dining area. This will also enable fast delivery of service.

5.1 Round tray or food tray   5.2 Bar tray   5.3 Rectangular tray

Catering Essentials: A guide to successful catering business

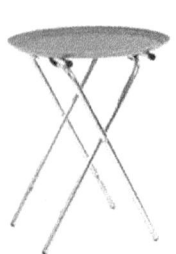

5.4 Jumbo tray/ Oval tray

5.5 Tray stands

6.   **Chafing dish**

6.1 Chafing dish/ Food warmer

(with complete parts: burner/ sterno, food pan, water pan and body)

6.2 Clear & Thick Soup warmer

7. Table centerpiece, Candelabras and Napery

7.1 Flower and Candelabra Centerpiece

7.2 Scallop Table Skirting

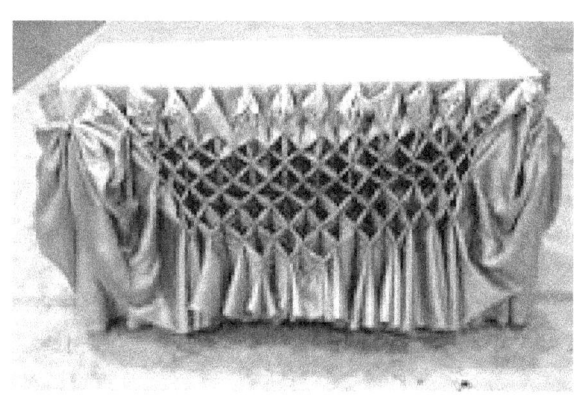 

7.3 Diamond Table Skirting   7.4 Table cloth with topper

Note: Guest's dining table should not be skirted to avoid pin injury.

Catering Essentials: A guide to successful catering business

Napkin folding

(source: luxelinen.org)

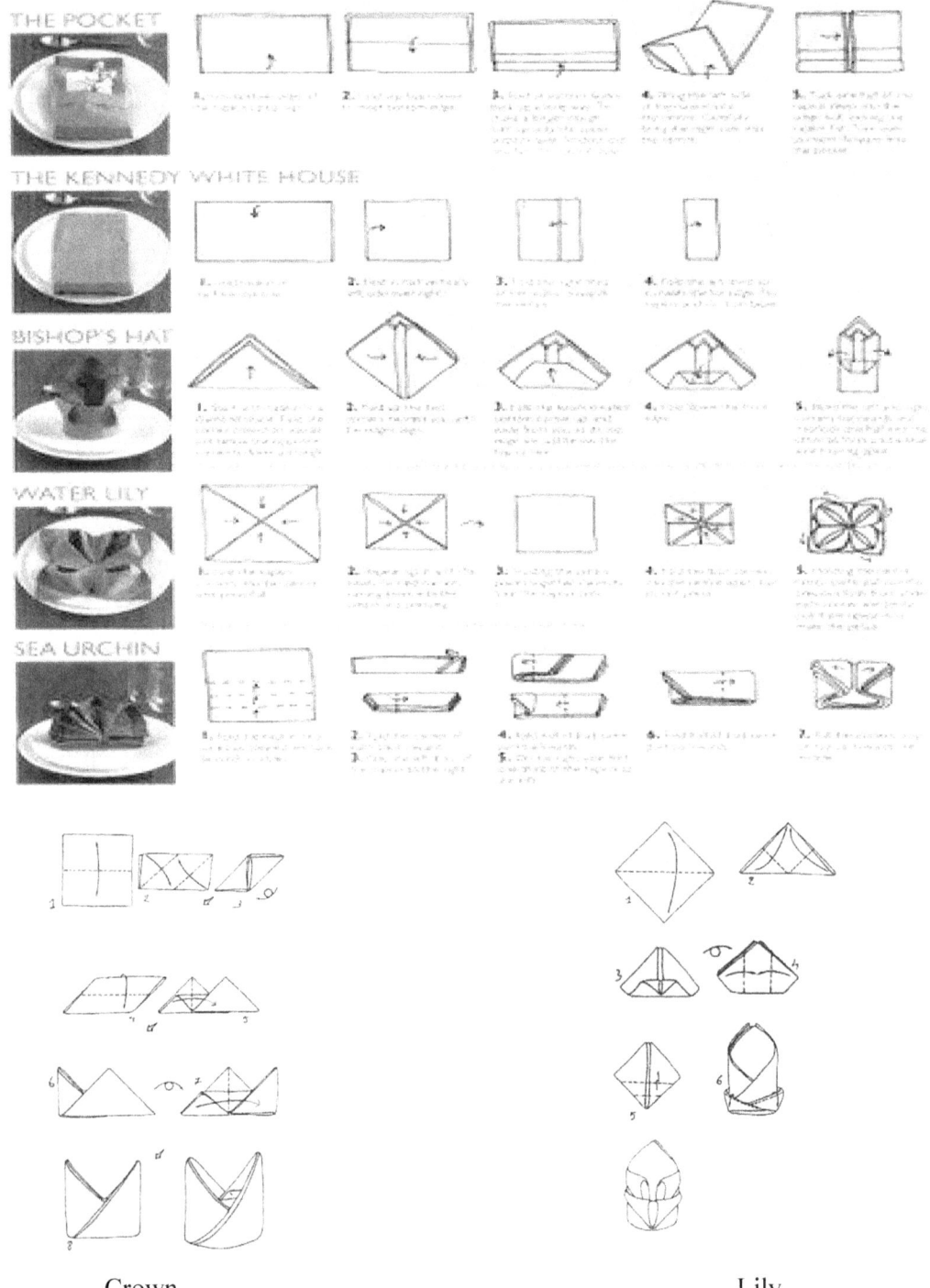

Crown   Lily

Catering Essentials: A guide to successful catering business

Manpower Requirements

There is a slight difference of manpower requirements between the Off- Premise and On-Premise Catering. On-premise catering means that the banquet service of the hotel handles venue set-up and food service for parties, wedding receptions, meetings and conferences.

On the other hand, Off-premise is providing food catering service to the different venues and sites preferred by the clients or organizers. This will need a competent driver for the vehicle that will transport the waitering staff, food, and service facilities to the venue.

The typical workforce of catering services

1.   Catering Service Manager

Reports to Catering Owner

Basic Function: Responsible in organizing, controlling, planning, and directing all catering related activities.

Specific Duties and Responsibilities:

1. Coordinates with the catering sales people about the profile and details of the function.
2. Identifies the number of waiters and service staff needed based on the preferred table service of the client or organizer.
3. Coordinates with the kitchen area for the on-time release of food and cross checks it with the function/event profile form.
4. Spearheads the preparation of utensils and equipment to be transported to the venue of the event.
5. Oversees the *mis-en-place* set-up of the venue.
6. Evaluates the performance of the waiters and other service staff as basis for

employment renewal.

7. Handles special guest request, complaints, and suggestions.

8. Prepares and submits report to the catering owner.

2. Head Chef

Reports to Catering Service Manager

Basic Function: Responsible for menu planning, food costing, recipe standardization and quantification, strict observance of hygienic food preparations and appealing presentation of food to guests.

Specific Duties and Responsibilities:

1. Oversees work activities of cooks and kitchen runners.

2. Prepares supply requisition.

3. Checks the quality and quantity of supplies delivered.

4. Implement and monitor food hygiene, sanitation, and safety.

5. Conduct food tasting and panel evaluation.

6. Coordinates with catering sales agents in formulating pre-design catering packages.

7. Employs food cost control techniques and considers creative ingredient options without sacrificing the quality of food.

3. Cook

Reports to Head Chef

Basic Function: Responsible of food preparation in accordance to the standardize recipes.

Specific Duties and Responsibilities:

1. Cooks food based on the menu preferred by the client/event organizer.

Catering Essentials: A guide to successful catering business

2. Observes hygienic food preparations.
3. Completes food production on-time.

4. Catering Waiter

Reports to Catering Service Manager

Basic Function: Responsible for the *mis-en-place* preparations and servicing of food in accordance to the service standards.

Specific Duties and Responsibilities:
1.   Sets up the food service venue based on the function/event profile form.
    1.1 dining tables and chair arrangements
    1.2 table set-up
    1.3 polishing of silver ware
    1.4 Set-up buffet stations *(if buffet service is preferred)*
2.   Serves food and beverage to guest if set-down menu is preferred.
3.   Answers customer's query about food.

5. Catering Sales Representative

Reports to Catering Service Manager

Basic Function: Responsible for catering sales and bookings.

Specific Duties and Responsibilities:
1. Handles inquiries regarding packages, menu, price etc.
2. Creates pre-design catering packages for various occasions and prepares proposal to clients/ organizers.
3. Discusses contract provisions with the client/ organizers.
4. Prepares the catering event profile form and furnish a copy to the manager and head chef.
5. Prepares and submits reports to the management.

===

Key terms

1. Pax
2. Pre-designed catering package
3. Mis-en-place
4. Napery
5. Table skirting
6. Food hygiene

===

Discussion Questions

1. Why do we have to be fully equipped with facilities? Justify your answer.
2. What are the styles in setting up buffet stations? Enumerate succinctly.
3. What are the qualifications for the catering manpower? Create a list and discuss each qualification.

===

Catering Essentials: A guide to successful catering business

References

Brown, G. and Hepner, K. (2009). Waiter's Handbook (4th edition). Australia: Pearson Australia Group PTY.

Frey, S. D. (2008). Off-premise Catering: Guidelines to Starting a Small Business. Print.

Hansen, B. and Thomas, C. (2005). Off-premise Catering Management. Hoboken, NJ: Wiley.

Hillman, H. (2003). The New Kitchen Science: A Guide to Knowing the Hows and Whys for Fun and Success in the Kitchen. Boston: Houghton Mifflin.

Hornsey, T. and Dann, D. T. (1984). Manpower Management in the Hotel and Catering Industry. London: Batsford.

Manpower Changes in the Hotel and Catering Industry. (1983). Wembley: Hotel and Catering Industry Training Board.

Napkin Folds. Available at http/www.luxelinen.org/tag/napkin-folds

Off-premise Catering How to Plan and Execute Large-scale Catered Events. (2015) John Wiley & Sons.

Roldan, A. S. and Edica, B. (2008). Food Service and Bartending (Revised Edition). Philippines: AR Skills Development and Management Services Publishing.

Schmidt, A. (2001). The Banquet Business. Weimar, TX: Chips.

Catering Essentials: A guide to successful catering business

The Maya Kitchen. (2004). Food service and Catering Management: A practical guide. Pasig City: Anvil Publishing House.

.

Chapter 4

Catering Service Package

Learning Objectives

1. Discuss the need of a customized catering package.
2. Execute correct recipe scale-up.
3. Explore the reasons on availing the services of a caterer.
4. Solve catering package computation.

To have a better grasp on the very essence of this business, let us use the business model canvas by answering the following questions.

1. What catering packages are we offering to our customer segments?
2. Which of the customer needs are we going to satisfy?
3. For whom are we creating the catering package?

Customer Segments & Catering Package Match

1. Academe
   The different colleges and universities customarily hold events like acquaintance parties, graduation balls, and promenades which are participated in by most students. They also conduct trainings, seminars, and workshops which are always attended by the different academic groups within the vicinity of the local area or to a national and international delegation.
   Product match: Banquet, meetings & seminar catering packages

2. Local Government Units
   Most of the time the Local Government Units (LGUs) have scheduled meetings and conferences every now and then. These activities are usually attended by directors, office heads, and rank and file employees.
   Product match: meetings, conferences and seminar catering packages

3. Non-Governmental Organizations
   Meetings and conference activities of non-Governmental Organizations (NGOs) which are non-profit and are often called civil societies of both national and international levels like the Women's Group, Red Cross, World Wildlife Fund,

International Organization for Standardization (ISO) and other related organizations are usually handled by a catering services.

Product match: meetings, conferences and seminar catering packages

4. Business Organizations

For Business Organizations, activities that require catering service include launching of new products, general meetings, product and service trainings, seminars, workshops and all other related activities.

Product match: meeting, conferences and seminar catering packages

5. Wedding, Debut and Birthday Parties

People nowadays are attuning to modern practice in dealing with gatherings and family events. Because of utmost preparation and considerable time allocated, they prefer to have their events be handled by catering services so as to save time, effort, and planning.

Product match: Banquet catering package

Meet and Satisfy Customers' needs

These are the reasons on why they have preferred to avail the services of a caterer.

1. Hassle Free

The organizing party does not need to worry on the preparation. The caterer almost does it all – from the physical set-up of the venue to the servicing of food to guests and attendees. Waitering staff should be well trained on how to provide table service and be able to execute details found in the Catering Event Profile Form.

2. Food Hygiene

Prospect clients avail of the catering services because of the hygienically prepared food. Since there are events which are attended by VIPs, dignitaries and other famous public figures, meticulous food preparation shall be observed to avoid embarrassment and disappointment. Also, good grooming of waitering staff must be part of the over-all hygiene of catering services.

3. Complete Food Service Facilities

A complete set of service facilities in the venue impresses the catering clients, guests and other attendees. Seeing these facilities is visually appealing to them such as the food warmers are in complete parts and well-polished; silver ware, dinner ware and glass ware designs are in uniform; and table napkins, table cloths and skirting cloths are clean and fresh.

4. Customer Care

It is only through catering service that the catering clients, guests, and other attendees of the events are specially taken care off. Somehow, there is a personalized care for each of them. Caterers have patience with difficult guests. They are tactful in words, sensitive to the guests' needs, knowledgeable on the product and are good in handling complaints and concerns.

Customized Catering Package

''There is no one-size-fits-all''. This saying simple means that you need to create a catering package that answers only to specific requirements of the client. For example, the needs of a debut party event is different from the needs of a seminar or a workshop perhaps. Tailoring to specific needs of the event enables the caterer to be fully effective in servicing the clients.

Quantity Food Production

Large scale food production is common in catering services. This usually happens during events that have bulk number of attendees especially if the occasion is important or seasonal. During this time, sometimes, the volume of preparation is not enough for the number of available food service staff which results to poor service and customer dissatisfaction. One funny story in some small catering services about their food production is they simply get figures in the air or just a gut feeling for the total weights of ingredients needed in food preparation. The outcomes of these poor practices are inconsistencies of taste, portions, color, and texture.

From a single recipe to large scale production, consistency of food quality is very necessary in order to retain customer satisfaction and to guard against unfavorable food expense. Consistency also builds trust and confidence among customers. With these two, you are establishing a great reputation in your catering service. The many satisfied customers are, the bigger chances of getting a word-of-mouth advertisement.

If standardized recipes and cost are already established, then we are ready for the large quantity of food production by following these simple guidelines: Familiarize measurement and conversion and do not deviate from the standardized recipes and established cost.

Measurements and Conversions

Basically, we measure solid in grams / kilo and liquid in ml. / liter

1/4 cup	= 60 gms.
	= 62.50 ml
	= 4 tbsps.
1/2 cup	= 120 gms.
	= 125 ml
	= 8 tbsps.
1 cup	= 240 gms.
	= 250 ml.
	=16 tbsps.
1 tsp.	= 5 gms.
1 tbsp.	= 15 gms.
	= 3 tsps.

Recipe Scale-up

Name of Recipe: Chicken Asado
Standard Yield: 5 servings
Desired number of yield: 50 servings

Ingredients	Measurements			TOTAL WEIGHTS NEDEED
	Standard quantity	Equivalent weights	multiplier	
Chicken	1 kg	1000 grams	X 10	10,000 grams / 10 kls.
Soy sauce	2 tbsps.	30 ml.		300 ml.
Calamansi juice	1/4 cup	62.50 ml.		625 ml.
Tomato sauce	1 1/2 cup	375 ml.		3,750 ml./ 3 liters and 750ml.
Onion	1 pc.	1 pc.		10 pcs.
Dried bay leaves	2 pcs.	2 pcs.		20 pcs.
Salt	1/2 teaspoon	2.5 grams		25 grams
Black pepper	1 tsp.	5 grams		50 grams
Water	1 cup	250 ml.		2,500 ml. or 2 1/2 liters

Here's how to get the multiplier

$$Multiplier = \frac{Desired\ number\ of\ yield}{Standard\ yield}$$

$$\frac{50}{5} = 10\ Multiplier$$

In weighing the ingredients, calibrated weighing scale should be used to arrive at the accurate amount. Sensory evaluation of weights is not advisable. All measuring tools for ingredients are cleaned, sanitized and ready for use.

For set-down table service like Russian and Plated, always scale up the recipes based on the number of pax stated in the catering event profile form. If buffet service is preferred, you add 10 to 15 percent buffet margin to the desired number of yield to prevent shortage of food.

Scaled-up recipe food costing

Name of Recipe: Chicken Asado
Standard Yield: 5 servings
Desired number of yield: 50 servings

Ingredients	Standard quantity	Unit cost	Final cost
Chicken	1 kg = 1000 grams	P 110.00/ 1000 grams	P 110.00
Soy sauce	2 tbsps.= 30 ml.	P 18.00/ 100 ml.	P 5.40
Lemonade	1/4 cup = 62.50 ml.	P 30.00/ 200 ml.	P 9.37
Tomato sauce	1 1/2 cup = 375 ml.	P 55.00/ 250 ml.	P 82.50
Onion	1 piece	P 3.00/ piece	P 3.00
Dried bay leaves	2 pieces	P 1.00/ piece	P 2.00
Salt	1/2 teaspoon = 2.5 grams	P 10.00/ 250 grams	P .01
Black pepper	1 tsp. = 5 grams	P 25.00/ 100 grams	P1.25
Water	1 cup	-	-
Total Food Cost = P 213.53			

Multiplier: 50 servings/ 5 servings = **10**

Let's compute the cost of 50 servings

Total Food Cost X Multiplier

P 213.53 X 10 = **P 2, 135.30** cost of 50 servings

Food cost is accurate if you based the unit cost of ingredients from the prevailing market prices. It is important to be always updated with the ingredient prices and make adjustments in your food cost records if there are changes.

If there is a big leap of price increase in one of the ingredients, substitutes are necessary, for as long as it will not affect the quality of food.

Catering Menu Costing

Chicken Asado	**P 2, 135.30**
Sweet and Sour Fish fillet	P 1, 785.00
Vietnamese Spring rolls	P 1, 380.00
Shanghai Fried Rice	P 1, 070.00
Chocolate Moist Cake	P 1, 150.00
Four Seasons Mocktail	P 670.00

Total Food Cost for 50 pax	=	P 8,190.30
Food Cost per pax	=	P 8,190.30/ 50 pax
	=	**P 163.80**

Operational Costs

3 Waiters at P300.00 each	P	900.00
4 cooks at P450.00 each	P 1,	800.00
2 kitchen runners	P	400.00
Ice Cubes	P	150.00
Driver	P	250.00
Petroleum Gas tanks	P	800.00
Total	P 4,	300.00

Package inclusions

Welcome streamer	P	300.00
Flower centerpieces	P 1,	300.00
3 layer Debut Cake	P 1,	000.00
Vanity wall	P	700.00
Total	P 3,	300.00

Package Computation

Sample computation of Debut Party Catering Package

Catering Menu Total Food Cost 50 pax   =   P 8,190.30
       Food Cost per pax   =   P 163.80

Let's compute the initial selling price using the factor pricing method mentioned in chapter 2.

P 213.53 X Factor (*ideal food cost percentage is from 24- 34 percent*)

If 28% = 100/ 28= 3.57 then P 163. 80 X 3.57 = P 584.77 initial selling
If 30% = 100/ 30= 3.33   then P 163.80 X 3.33 = P 545.45 initial selling
If 33% = 100/33= 3.03 then P 163.80 X 3.03 = P 496.31 initial selling

Initial selling price X 50 pax

If the desired food cost percentage is 33%
   P 496. 31
      + 10% service charge *(P49.63)*
      + (10% buffet margin - only for eat all you can menu)
   ==
   P 545.94
      X 50 pax
   ================
   P 27, 297.00 + P 4, 300.00 (operational cost) + P 3, 300.00 (inclusions)

   P 34, 897.00 total cost of package

   P34, 897.00 / 50 pax = P 697.94 Selling price per pax
                          or can be rounded off P 698.00

Catering Essentials: A guide to successful catering business

1.1 Sample of Debut Catering Package Proposal

Greppoo Catering Services
www.greppoo.com.ph
Telefax 032-521-43-55
'Service is our business'

Debut Catering Package

Inclusions
Plated Menu
Welcome streamer
3 layer debut cake
Floral Arrangement as table centerpiece
Free flowing coffee or tea
Free of corkage for the first two bottles of champagne
Free of corkage for 1 Roasted Turkey
Free use of Public Address System

At P698.00 per pax for a minimum of 50 pax

1.2 Debut Party Menu Sample

Menu
(Plated Service)

Chicken Asado

Sweet and Sour Fish fillet

Vietnamese Spring rolls

Shanghai Fried Rice

Chocolate Moist Cake

Four Seasons Mocktail

Coffee or tea

1.3 Letter Proposal Sample

Greppoo Catering Services
www.greppoo.com.ph
Telefax 032-521-43-55
'Service is our business'

July 23, 2016

DR. MODESTA ALONSO
Head, ABC Cooperative
Sikatuna St., Cebu City

Dear Doctor Alonso:

What a proud moment in your life that your one and only daughter will be 18 years old next month! It is a moment to be treasured -an event to be looked back upon as the years rolled by- above all, an event to be celebrated.

It is my pleasure and privilege to present to you a catering proposal for the debut party of your daughter on August 25, 2016, Debut Banquet for 50 pax at 35th Street, corner Saturn Project 5, Cebu City.

Attached are the details for your perusal and consideration. I shall be pleased to arrange an appointment at your convenience, or call us at 032-521-43-55.

Greppoo Catering is looking forward to be of service to you especially in celebrating memorable occasions in your family.

Sincerely,

MS. NIKKA LABASTIDA
Catering Manager

1.4 Catering Agreement/ Event Profile Form Sample

Name of Organizer _____
Residential Address: _____
Office Address: _____
Contact numbers
     Cellphone _____
     Land line _____

Reservation Date: _____
Date of function: _____ Day_____ Time _____
Menu:

        _____
        _____
        _____

Inclusions/ Amenities

        _____
        _____

Table Service
        Buffet ( )   Russian ( )   Plated ( )
Special Arrangements (additional round of drinks, Cake, Mobile Bar, etc.)

        _____
        _____
        _____
        _____

Set-up/ Venue Lay-out Instructions and number of persons in the presidential table

        _____
        _____
        _____

Minimum Guarantee of pax/ guest _____
Cost per Pax _____
Total Cost _____
Amount Deposit_____
Balance _____ Payable on _____

Contracting party: _____
                Signature over printed name
Date_____
Catering Sales Account Executive _____
                   Signature over printed name
Date _____

1.5 Terms and Conditions Sample
(Usually printed at the back part of the Catering event profile form)

Catering Terms and Conditions

1. A 50 % payment of deposit should be made upon reservation
       30% partial payment 5 days prior to the event date
       20% remaining balance should be settled upon the completion of
       service. All payments are cash basis.

2. Catering package adjustment or modification requests should be made one week before the date of the event.

3. Cancellation is valid a week before the confirmed date of the event and subject to 25% cancellation fee to defray preparation cost of the caterer. Cancellation less than one week will forfeit the down-payment made.

4. Food and beverage served by the caterer remains caterer's property, take-out food practices is being discouraged. Special considerations can be given if the actual count of pax is lower than the minimum guaranteed.

5. Breakages or losses of caterer's service wares will be charged to the organizer unless due to waitering staff negligence.

6. The caterer will service the event for a maximum of 4 hours only. Should you need extensions, an extra amount shall be paid since this can prevent the caterer from cleaning and removing of service equipment.

Signatures over printed name:

_____   _____
    Contracting Party   Caterer

Note:

The sample 1.4 and 1.5 serves as legal agreement between the organizer and the caterer. Furnish a copy of Catering event Profile Form to the office of the catering manager, Head Chef and the Head Waiter for their guidance and quick reference.

1.6 Sample of Wedding Banquet Catering Package

Greppoo Catering Services
www.greppoo.com.ph
Telefax 032-521-43-55
'Service is our business

Wedding Catering Package

Buffet Menu
1 Roasted beef
Guest book
5-layer wedding cake
Flower Arrangements and centerpieces
A pair of Wedding doves
A choice of wedding souvenir (60 pcs)
Free of corkage for the first two bottles of champagne
Free use of Public Address System

At P750·00 per pax for a minimum of 100 pax

1.7 Sample of Conference- Meeting Package

Greppoo Catering Services
www.greppoo.com.ph
Telefax 032-521-43-55
'Service is our business'

Conference- Meeting Package

Inclusions

Luncheon Buffet Menu
Note pads with pencil
Nuts and chips
Welcome streamer
Free Flowing Coffee and Tea
Public Address System
LCD Projector
Registration table with guest book

At P750·00 per pax for a minimum of 100 pax

==

Key terms

1. Customer care
2. Banquet
3. Scale up
4. Contracting party
5. Pax
6. Event profile

==

I- Discussion Questions

1. Create a catering package for baptismal reception.
2. Enumerate the steps in recipe scale-up.
3. Discuss ways on how you can convince the client to avail catering services.
4. Explain why there is a 10% service charge part of the package computation.

II- Simulate these catering events

Create a Catering Package for Children's Party (50 pax)
* Menu (food costing & recipe scale-up)
* Package Inclusions
* Package Price
* Proposal letter

Create a Catering Package for ABC Board Meeting (30pax)
* Menu (food costing & recipe scale-up)
* Package Inclusions
* Package Price
* Proposal letter

Create a Catering Package for Golden Wedding Anniversary (100pax)
* Menu (food costing & recipe scale-up)
* Package Inclusions
* Package Price
* Proposal letter

References

Careers Speaker's Package. (1981). Wembley: Hotel & Catering Industry Training Board.

Ketterer, M. (1991). How to Manage a Successful Catering Business. New York: Van Nostrand Reinhold.

Monitoring Catering Revenue & Costs: Trainee Workbook. (1997). Melbourne, Vic.: Australian Training Products.

Packer, B. C. (n.d.). Catering Business: How to Start & Manage Your Very Own Catering Business.

Packer, B. C. (2013). Catering Business: How to Start, Operate and Be Successful with Your Very Own Catering Business. Not Mentioned: Bowe Chaim Packer.

Start Your Own Catering Business. (1995). Johannesburg: Pfeiffer.

The Catering Business. (2000). London: Mintel International Group.

Turner, M. and Evans, A. (1995). Menu Costing Using a Spreadsheet: Work Based Project Using a Computer. Bristol: Further Education Staff College.

Vivaldo, D. (n.d.). How to Start a Home-based Catering Business. n.p.

Chapter 5
Table Services in Catering

Learning Objectives

1. Explain the importance of *mise-en-place* preparation.
2. Familiarize table set-up procedures.
3. Identify the types of table services used in catering.
4. Enumerate the types of meeting room lay-out.

Mise-en-place in Food Service

Mise-en-place is putting everything in one place. The food service brigade should be at the function hall or at the event area at least 3 hours for the mise-en-place preparations. Successful execution of food service strongly depends on the correctness of the set-up, on-time completion, and skilled food service staffs. The guide in setting up the venue such as dining table arrangements, lay-out, type of table service etc. can be seen in catering event profile form.

Mise-en-place Guidelines

1.   Request and prepare the serving tools needed in food service. The menu in the Catering Event Profile Form will give you an idea on the serving gears to be prepared. Polish all the silver wares, china wares and glass wares with clean and dry cloth and must be piled properly to avoid accidental breakages.

2.   In the off-premise catering, make sure all service tools, utensils, equipment and foods are loaded and neatly arranged in the delivery van. Double check the items with the event profile making sure nothing is left behind. The driver should check the vehicle conditions like tire and other spare parts to avoid delay. Be sure to arrive at the venue early so that you will have ample time for the set-up.

3.   The number of waiters are based on the productivity ratio. Shortage of manpower could cause slow service and inconveniences.

4.   Check good grooming of waiters, uniform is ironed, nail cut short, hair is trimmed, not using heavy or strong perfumes and no jewelry. The food service staffs are your front liners, they should look good and presentable.

5.   Follow the floor plan details found in the special instructions of the event profile form. Be sure there is enough clearance from one table to provide ease to waiters in serving foods and dish-outing.

6.   Table Setting. The space and the distance of the table set-up from the next table set-up is 24" to 30" wide. This is done to prevent seated guests hitting each other elbow to elbow. Follow the standards table set-up;

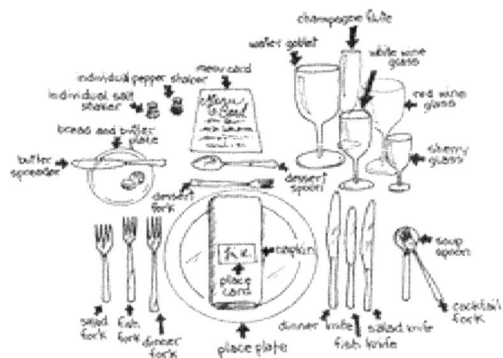

Note: The salad knife, fish knife, and dinner knife, soup spoon and appetizer fork should be at the right side of the cover. The Dinner fork, fish fork, and salad fork should be at the left side of the cover. The bread and butter plate with the bread and butter knife are set at the upper left of the forks. The glasses are placed on the upper part of the knives.

Follow the menu list in the event profile form. Example: if there is no fish in the menu list, then omit the fish fork and fish knife. Do not set the cutlery if not needed.

In buffet service, dinner plates are placed at the buffet station. What you will set on the table are the dinner knife and dinner fork with table napkin at the center of the cover. While the water goblet set half inch from the tip of the dinner knife.

Distance of the Silver wares from the edge of the table is at least 1 inch. Always remember, set only cleaned, sterilized, and polished cutleries on the table.

Table centerpiece should something that is below the eye level and not huge, so that it won't disrupt guests' conversation.

7.   Flower centerpiece should be set at presidential table. If there's a need to put tent cards and signages, check the spelling correctness before putting it on facing the public.

8. Check the condition of the audio- visual facilities.

9. Set up registration and cake table if stated in the event profile.

10. Set-up waiter station.

Table Services

Not all table services fit in catering services. The following are the most common types of table services adapted in by most of the catering.

1. Buffet

It is popularly known as ''eat-all-you-can'' and "self-service". This type of service does not need a lot of waiters. What the waiter will do is to dish-out plates if the guest is done with the food or if asked to do so.

In setting up of buffet station, it should be something that is appealing and appetizing to look at. Skirting cloths will add class in the set-up.

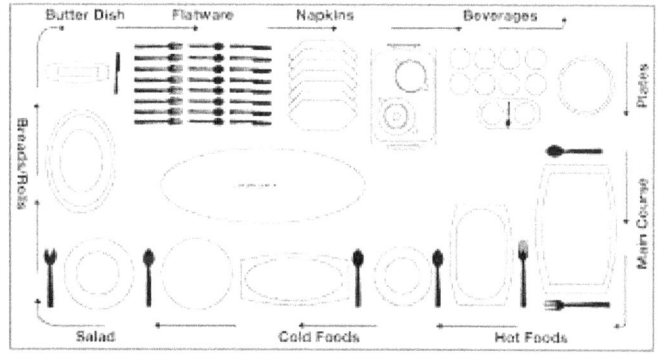

2. American Service/ Plated Service

This is the exact opposite of buffet. The food is pre-cut and arrange individually in the plates at the kitchen. This is one of the set-down menus. The waiter serves food to the individual guest seated and follows the standard meal sequence in serving: appetizer, soup, salad, side dish, main dish, and dessert. Serving it one at a time, clear the table to make way for the next dish. Ask permission politely before removing the plate. You may ask the following questions: *Are you done with the food sir/ma'am? May I remove the plate, so I can serve the next dish?*

The arrangement of food in the plate should be something that is appealing to guest when it is served on the table.

3.   Russian Service/ Silver Service

The waiter takes the food using silver platter and unload the food to the guest plate using spoon and fork as food clip. It is an elegant form of table service and would require highly skilled waiters.

The service is used especially in the highly ranked hotels, restaurants and in catering operations. In Russian service, the waiter place all the food items on a silver platter and arrange it attractively and present to guests for approval and serve the food on the left side.

Russian service utilizes too many silver wares and large platters while serving the guests.

Rules in Service

1.   Serve food with appropriate dinner ware and garnish.

2.   Serve food in the standard meal sequence -- from lightest to heaviest.

3.   Whenever you approach the guests on the table to serve them with food, please courteously say ''excuse me ma'am/sir'' to alert them and to prevent food and drinks from spilling.

4. Serve on the appropriate side of the guests. Do not serve across the guest, unless the situation prevents you to do so. Serve food from the right side *(Plated)*, serve food from the left side *(Russian)*.

5. When serving, always mention the name of the dish. *''Beef with onions Sir''*

6.   Serve the ladies first followed by the gentlemen. If there are children seated, serve them first.

7.   For hygienic reasons, hold the plate at the rim side by not touching the surface of the plate with your thumb.

8.   Never use cutlery that has fallen off on the floor.

9.   When transferring the food from one container to the other, always use tong and never hold it with your bare hands.

10.   Do not overload tray, bend you knees not your back when lifting loaded trays.

11. Presence of mind shall be observed while on service. Absent mindedness could cause accident in the service areas.

12. Hands on your buttocks when standing at the assigned service station.

13. In buffet service, while the food is waiting for the serving time, make sure the burners are working to maintain warmness of food.

15.   Prepare some pitchers with ice cold water in your stations.

16.   Use two or three way plate method in clearing the table.

 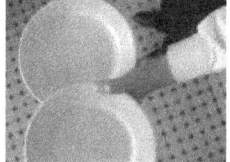

Sample of Banquet Area Lay-out
(wedding)

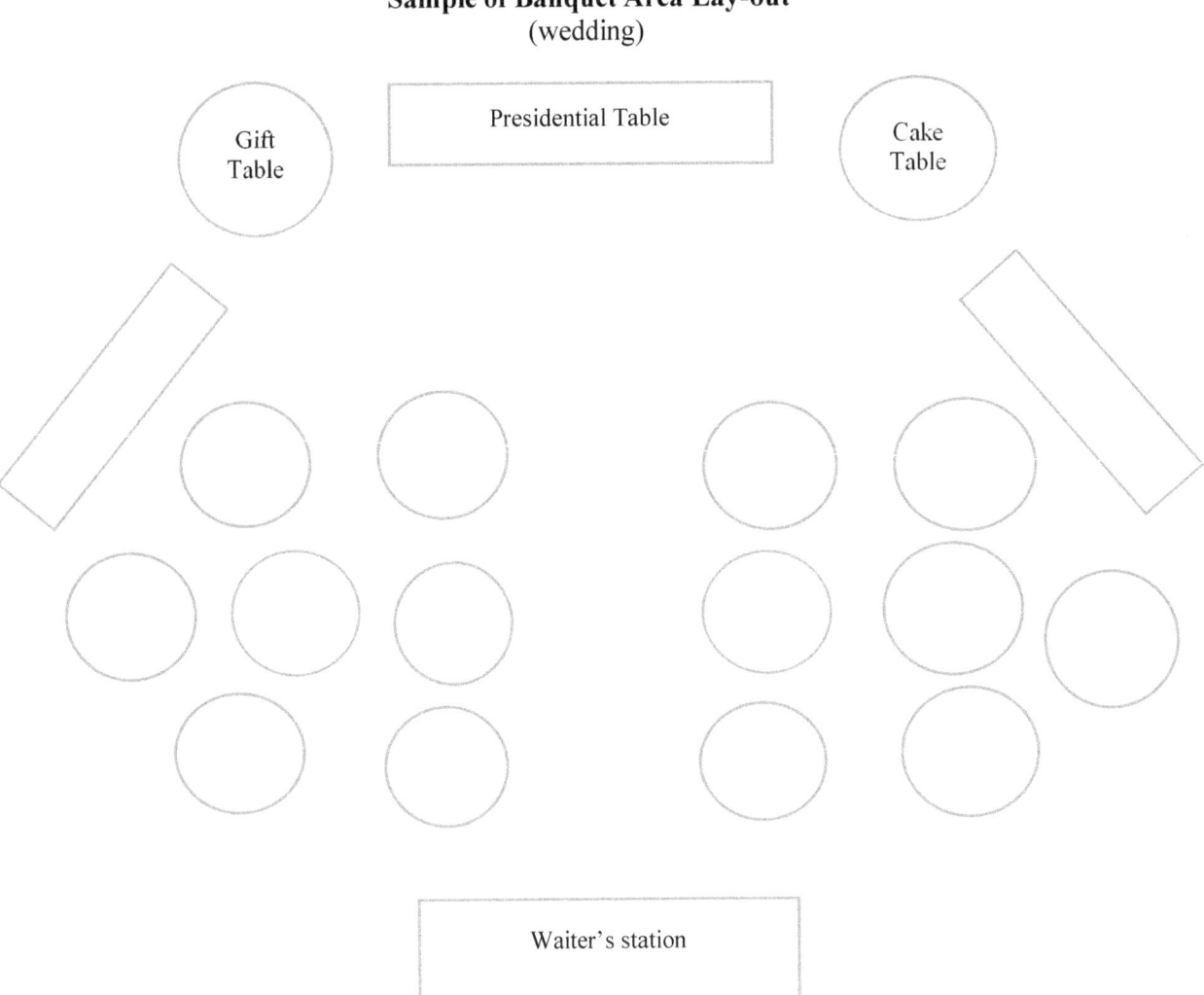

Note:

To prevent overcrowding of buffet station. The ratio is 1 buffet station for every 50 guests. In large banquet gatherings like 200 pax, the event organizer is given small color coded ribbon to distribute it to the arriving guest. The ribbon corresponds to the color of the buffet table skirting cloth.

The caterer should lessen the inconveniences in buffet service by following the ratio. Shortage of buffet stations is the most common source of complaints.

The waiter should actively refill foods in the food warmer/ chafing dish, and assign 1 serving spoon in each food item to avoid blending of food flavors. Make sure that the chafing dish burner/ sterno is working to maintain food warm.

Catering Essentials:A guide to successful catering business

Sample Lay-outs of Meeting/ Conference

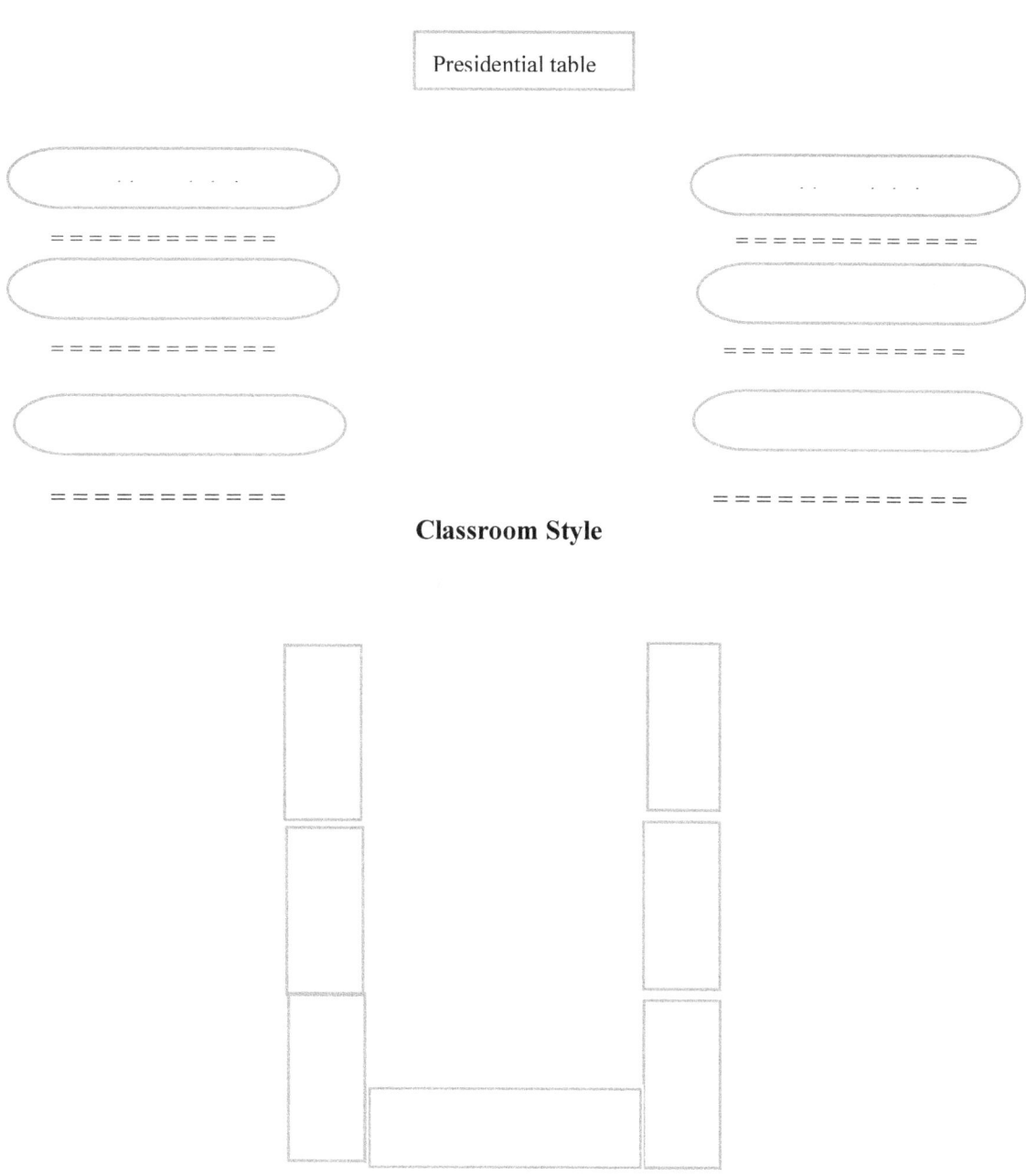

Presidential table

Classroom Style

U-shape style

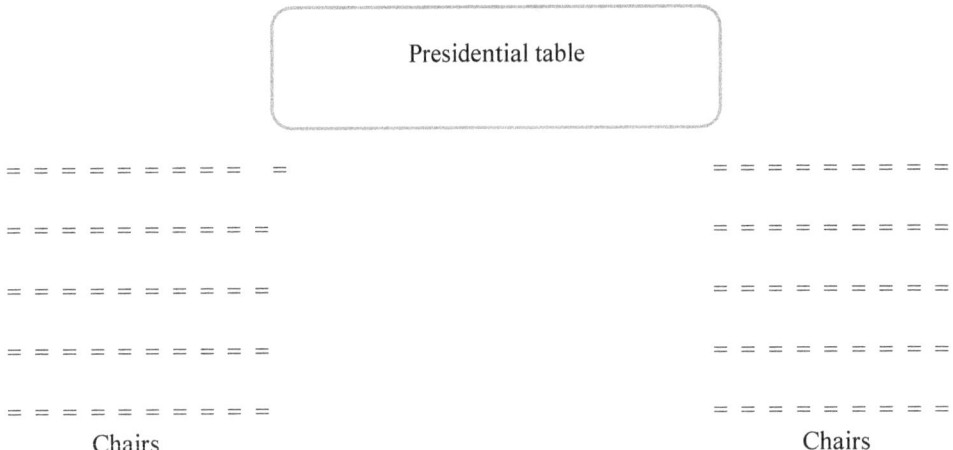

Theater Style

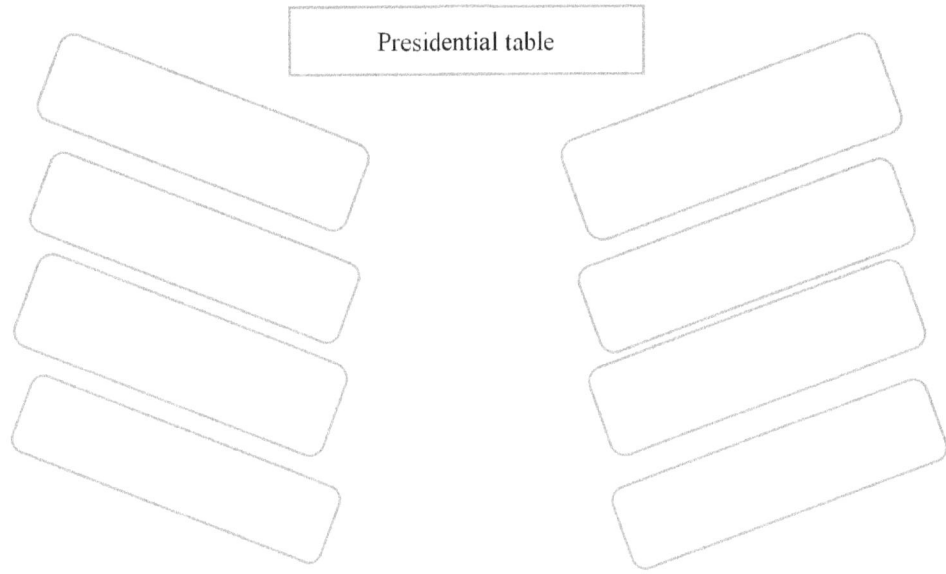

Fish bone style

Activities after the catering event

1. After the end of the function, checking and counting of service wares should be done, take note of breakages and losses. Locate missing items, (under the chairs, tables etc) If the function is an off-premise, missing items should be relayed to the organizer for them to assist in locating the missing items.

2.   As stipulated in the contract, the organizer will be fined for the breakages caused by guests. If negligence of the waitering staff, disciplinary action can be taken.

3.   Left overs are deposited in black bags and should be disposed properly. Soiled dishes should be compiled neatly (scrap, stock, segregate). Used glasses are compiled on the glass racks to avoid cracks and breakages.

4.   Borrowed cutleries from the store room should be cross checked with the record and return promptly after use.

5.   Remove all crumbs from the table cloths and napkins, fold or bundle them properly. Extra careful in skirting cloths, pins and thumbtacks are removed first before folding them neatly.

6.   Remove tables & chairs unlock all stackable ones, fold and compile them at the store room or stack them neatly in the vehicle in the case of the off-premise catering.

7.   Avoid overloading of tray when dish outing as this would cause accident and injury.

8.   Clean the floor area by picking up pieces of papers and other litters.

9.   Ask guest to spend a little time in answering comments/ suggestions sheets. This is the best way to improve the quality of service.

==

Key Terms

1. Mise-en-place
2. Theater style
3. Classroom style
4. Fishbone style
5. Dish outing
6. Russian service
7. American service

==

Discussion Questions

1. What is *mise-en-place*?
2. What are the rules in table setting?
3. What are the types of table services are popularly used in catering services?
4. What meeting room lay-out that is appropriate to small meetings?

==

References

Alouche, J. (1988). How to Be Successful in a Food Service Operation: Waiter's Handbook. Don Mills, Ont.: J. Alouche

Brown, G. and Kepner, K. (2009). The Waiter's Handbook (4th edition). Pearson Education South Asia Pte Ltd.

Brown, G. and Kepner, K. (1993). The Waiter's Handbook. Melbourne: Hospitality

Fuller, J. (1986). Essential Table Service: For Restaurants: A New Version of the Standard Textbook the Waiter. London: Hutchinson

Lillicrap, D. R (1988). Revision Questions on Food and Beverage Service. London: Edward Arnold

Chapter 6

Food Safety

Learning Objectives

1. Explain the importance of food safety in catering.
2. Identify food hazards and its effect.
3. Describe the time and temperature abuse.
4. Distinguish the effects of cross contamination.

Importance of food Safety

Food poisoning has been rampant in small food establishments particularly because its food service staff lacks the training on preparing the food safely and securely. Hygienically prepared food is one of the secrets to success in food business since people nowadays are very meticulous in the aspect of sanitation and hygiene most especially in the food they eat.

It is part of the customer care to provide not only appetizing food to the customers but a safer food for consumption. Trust and loyalty are earned from them once they see that the food preparation, presentation, and service have observed strict hygiene and sanitary measures. Quality of food is not only the basis for customer satisfaction.

We heard a lot of food poisoning stories and victims suffered so much due to restaurant negligence. In the United States, some of the food service establishments were penalized due to food poisoning cases. There were some food service establishments in the Philippines are sued due to food poisoning. Now, food service establishments are so careful because they learned it in a hard way.

Proper food safety training to food service employees should be one of the top priorities of the food entrepreneur. You may tap the nearest Department of Health to give you enough training on Food Hygiene, Sanitation and Safety. DOH is also the granting agency of Sanitary Permit of the food service establishments. Food Safety training should not end by the giving of training certificates alone, it should be put into practice, strict implementation, monitoring and evaluation. Just make sure, the one that implements food safety has a deep understanding about the matter.

Food Safety Hazards

Hazard is a source of danger and they are being categorized into three namely; Biological Hazard, Physical Hazard and Chemical Hazard. Let's tackle the details of these hazards and identify some techniques to prevent or lessen the probability of occurrence.

Biological Hazard

Biological hazard are the microorganisms such as bacteria, fungi, viruses and parasites. Microorganism develop and multiplies rapidly in the temperature danger zone from **5 degree Celsius to 60 degree Celsius.** Potentially hazardous foods are meats and proteinous foods (egg, milk & cheese). Meat cooked foods should be placed in food warmers while waiting for the serving time and maintain the holding temperature of at least 61 degree Celsius to 64 degree Celsius. While cold foods (salads) should be in the freezer with a temperature below 5 degree Celsius.

Time and Temperature abuse is a prolong exposure of food item to the temperature danger zone. Cooked food which is exposed to TDZ for 3 hours or more should not be served to guests. Re-heating of food that is already exposed to TDZ and

Catering Essentials: A guide to successful catering business

with early signs of spoilage is useless, only microorganism that is killed but the bacterial toxin/waste remains and enough to poison you.

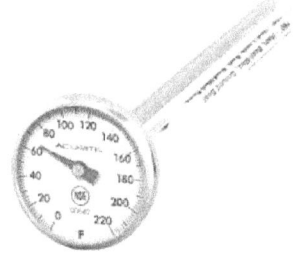

Dial-Face Food Thermometer

Steps on how to use food thermometer

1. Rub the censor stick of your thermometer with alcohol.
2. Calibrate your food thermometer by immersing the censor stick in the very hot or ice cold water.
3. Once the red hand points to zero, the thermometer is ready for use.

Factors that could spark biological hazards.

1.   *Buying of food supplies from unreliable sources.*

Supplier of meats, fish, fruits and vegetables should be someone that you can trust. Meat (pork, chicken and beef) should passed the meat inspection requirements of the Veterinary or from a HACCP certified slaughtering plant, and frozen when it is delivered. Fish and other seafood products are also frozen when it is delivered. Fruits and vegetables has no signs of decay and bruises.

2.   *Freezers are malfunctioned and with no enough space and compartment.*

The size of your freezer dictates the volume of your purchases. Before storing meats and fish, use individual containers for each meat type to prevent cross contamination and pile them neatly in the freezer with label. To prolong life span of vegetables and fruits, place them in the non-freeze refrigerators.

3.   *Inappropriate food thawing*

Bacteria is inactive if it is frozen and multiplies fast when you defrost. Thaw only a portion of meat that you need in cooking, once thawed you cannot put it back to the freezer. Thaw fast, you may use microwave in thawing or soaked in a very hot water.

4.   *Using un-sanitized cooking utensils*

Cleaning is just a simple removing of visible dirt. Sanitizing is the process of eliminating the microorganism from the utensils. Utensils in the store room should be sanitized again before using them. You may use dish-washing paste with anti-bacterial properties or diluted chlorine.

5.   *No FIFO system (First-in First-out)*

No FIFO system is a high risk. This is one of the major causes of food poisoning. Checking expiration dates of can goods and other supplies and discard those expired ones. In FIFO system, it will save you from high food waste. Consume first the items which are close to expiry dates and place the newly purchased at the far side of the shelves.

6.   *One chopping board for all*

One chopping board for all increases the risk of cross contamination. The use of color coded chopping boards is appropriate.

Catering Essentials: A guide to successful catering business

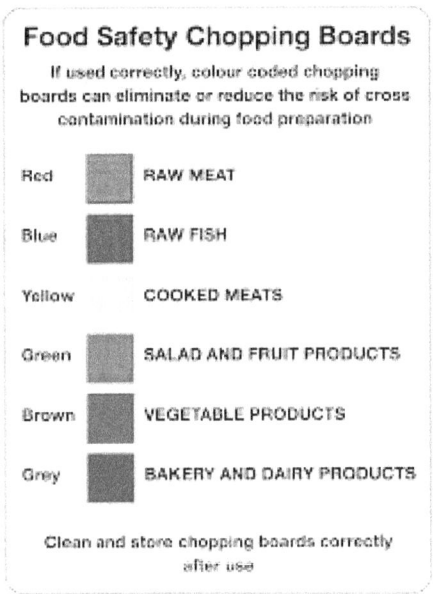

Color coded chopping boards

7. Food is not properly cooked.

A food that is not cook properly is not safe for consumption. Cook the food to these minimum end-point temperatures or higher. Use the calibrated thermometer to avoid over cooking.

Table 7.1 Cooking Guidelines (FDA, 2000)

Type of Food	Minimum Internal Temperature at Minimum Time before Serving
Poultry	74 degree Celsius for 15 seconds
Ground of flake meat	68 degree Celsius for 15 seconds
Pork	63 degree Celsius for 15 seconds
Roast Pork and Beef	63 degree Celsius for 4 minutes
Beef steaks and lamb	63 degree Celsius for 15 seconds
Fish	63 degree Celsius for 15 seconds
Vegetables	57 degree Celsius for 15 seconds (held above 57 degree Celsius)

8.   *Improper hand washing.*

Dirty hands is one of the sources of cross contamination. The kitchen personnel and food service staff should be acquainted with the proper hand washing.

Hand Washing Procedure (source: World Health Organization)

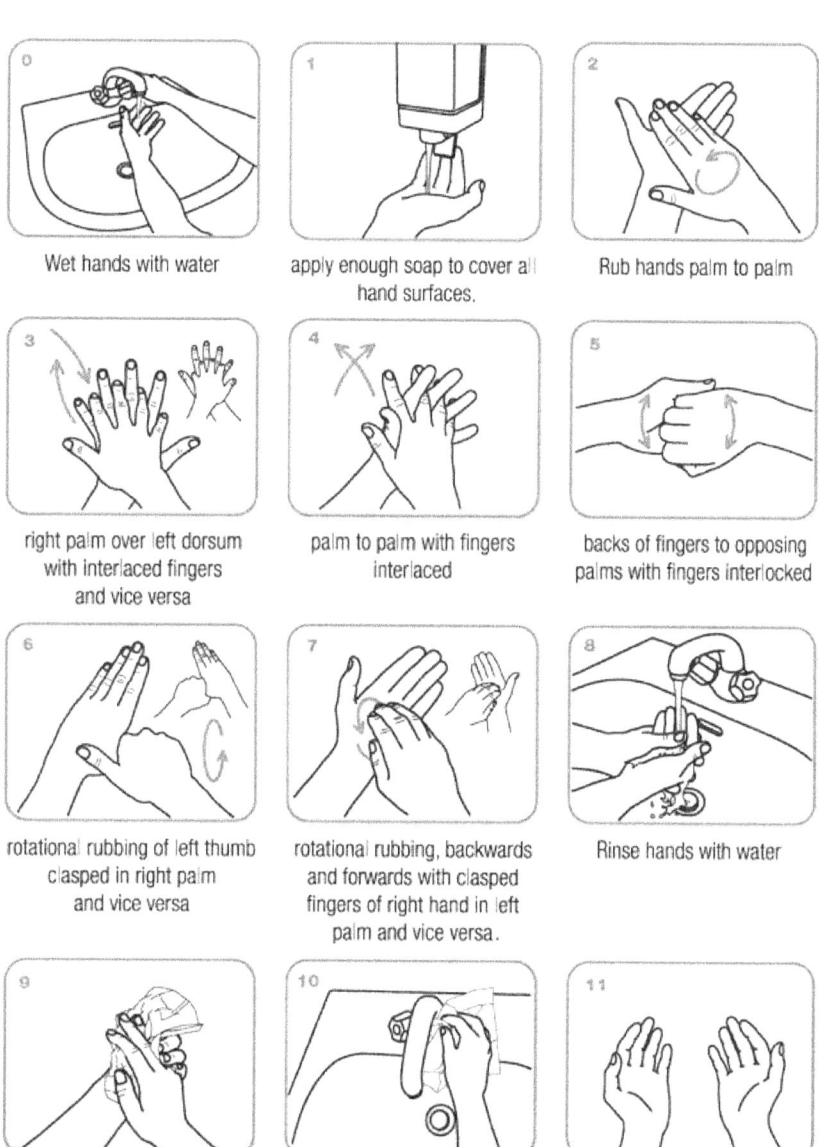

Wet hands with water	apply enough soap to cover all hand surfaces.	Rub hands palm to palm
right palm over left dorsum with interlaced fingers and vice versa	palm to palm with fingers interlaced	backs of fingers to opposing palms with fingers interlocked
rotational rubbing of left thumb clasped in right palm and vice versa	rotational rubbing, backwards and forwards with clasped fingers of right hand in left palm and vice versa.	Rinse hands with water
dry thoroughly with a single use towel	use towel to turn off faucet	...and your hands are safe.

Physical Hazard

Physical hazard are the foreign objects accidentally mixed in food like, hair, broken glasses, small metals (nail, blades, broken needles, staple wire etc.) and pieces of wood. These foreign objects are also a source of cross contamination. Small metals and pieces of wood could chock guest if accidentally swallowed and could lead to serious condition.

Factors that could spark physical hazards.

1.	*Not wearing of hairnet while working with food.*

A food with hair strand is very disgusting and shows that the catering is poor in hygiene and sanitation. Strict implementation of the wearing of hair net is a must.

2. *Construction materials are left behind after kitchen repairs.*

Small metals left behind in the kitchen work areas and accidentally mixed with food is disastrous. Food production should not resume unless all construction materials are completely removed.

3.	*Fruit peel and toothpicks accidentally mixed with food.*

This sometimes happen when everybody in the kitchen is rushing, but even so, presence of mind is very important so that we can always do things right.

4. *The cooked food left uncovered.*

If left uncovered, food is exposed to dust and flies. The food should be covered while waiting for the serving time.

5. *Small insects and rodents landed in food.*

Periodic visit of exterminator is necessary in order to eliminate all those sorts of insects and rodents and to destroy also their breeding grounds.

6. *Cloth, rugs and sponges accidentally fall into food.*

These items should be away from food. This will not happen if things in kitchen are organized.

Chemical Hazard

Chemical hazard are the cleaning chemicals such as chlorine, multipurpose cleaner, degreasers, solvents, pesticides, insecticides and etc. These items are fatal if large amount is accidentally mixed with food.

Factors that could spark Chemical Hazards.

1. *Chemical storage is within the kitchen area.*

The risk is very high if the chemical storage is within the kitchen area. Many of the food poisoning incidents are foods which are contaminated with chemicals.

Keep all chemicals away from the food production area. Isolate the chemical storage and keep them locked. Assign somebody as custodian for the release of the chemicals needed and appropriate amount.

2.   *Shellfish Toxins*

There are shellfish that contains toxins and could cause food poisoning such as mussels, oysters and scallops. If the red tide is alerted by the authorities, purchase of the said shellfish should be avoided.

3.   *Poisonous mushrooms*

Poisonous Mushrooms
(source: Dreamstime 2016)

Edible Mushrooms

(source: Food Source Information 2015)

White button

The most popular mushroom, white buttons represent about 90 percent of mushrooms consumed in the United States.

Crimini

Also known as baby 'bellas or browns, criminis are similar in appearance to whites, but have a light-tan to rich-brown cap and a firmer texture.

Portabella

A larger relative of criminis, Portabellas have tan or brown caps and measure up to 6 inches in diameter.

Shiitake

Shiitakes are tan to dark brown and have broad, umbrella-shaped caps, wide open veils, tan gills and curved stems that should be removed.

Oyster

Oysters can be gray, pale yellow or even blue, with a velvety texture.

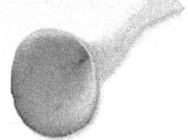

Enoki

Enoki have tiny, button-shaped caps and long, spindly stems.

Beech

Beech mushrooms are petite with either all-white or light-brown caps.

Maitake

Maitake appear rippling and fan-shaped, without caps. They are also called "Hen of the Woods."

==

Key terms

1.   TDZ

2.   FIFO

3.   Time and Temperature Abuse

4.   Toxins

5.   Biological Hazard

6.   Physical Hazard

7.   Chemical Hazard

==

Discussion Questions

1.   What is food safety?

2.   How do you prevent food hazards?

3.   How do you explain time and temperature abuse?

4.   Why is it that cross contamination occur?

==

Catering Essentials: A guide to successful catering business

References

Barber, M. (1978). Guidelines for Food Purchasing. Toronto: Ontario Hospital
    Association.

Bartos, J. (2011). Food Safety. Detroit: Greenhaven.

Center for Food Safety and Inspection Service USDA. Available at
    http://www.cfsan.fda.gov.

CleanHands Protection. Available at.
    http://www.who.int/gpsc/clean_hands_protection/en/lean_hands protection.

Food Source Information. Colorado Integrated Food Safety Center of Excellence
    Available at http://www.fsicolostate.edu.

Fraziner, W. and Westhoff, D. (2006). Food Microbiology (4th edition). New Delhi:
    Tata Mcgraw-hill.

Guide for Food Handlers: Food Safety and Hygiene. (1988). Montréal: Communauté.

Guillemoteau, J. (1987). Cross-Contamination: Study and Control: Round Table
    Discussion ; Memorandum and Conclusions. Berne.

Kearney, C. (2000). Food Hygiene for Food Handlers: A Primary Course in Food
    Hygiene for Food Workers. Wicklow Town: Environmental Health Officers'
    Association.

Lawley, R., Curtis, L. and Davis, J. (2008). The Food Safety Hazard Guidebook.
    Cambridge, UK: RSC Pub.

Catering Essentials: A guide to successful catering business

Poisonous Mushroom. Available at http://www.dreamstime.com.

Principles and Methods for the Risk Assessment of Chemicals in Food. (2009).
Geneva: World Health Organization.

Pulle, M. (2003). Food Hazards: Factors That Affect Food Safety. Sandgate, Qld:
Knowledge and Software.

Sheen, B. (2005). Food Poisoning. Detroit: Thomson/Gale.

Trickett, J. (1997). Food Hygiene for Food Handlers. Hound mills, Basingstoke,
Hampshire: Macmillan.

Glossary

Allergens- A substance that causes allergy.

Appetizer - A small dish of food (finger foods) served before the main part of the meal

Banquet- An elaborate and often ceremonious meal for numerous people often in honor of a person.

Biological Hazard- Also known as bio-hazards, refer to biological substances that pose a threat to the health of living organisms, primarily that of humans. This includes virus or bacterial toxin (from a biological source) that can affect human health.

Brunch- A meal that combines breakfast and lunch and that is usually eaten in the late morning.

Buffet- A meal set out on a buffet table or table for ready to access and informal service.

Catering- To provide food and drinks at a party, meeting, etc.

Celsius- Relating to or having a scale for measuring temperature on which the boiling point of water is at 100 degrees and the freezing point of water is at 0 degrees.

Chafing dish- A dish that is used for warming food at the table.

Chemical Hazard- Is a ny substance that can cause harm, primarily to people. Household chemical such as chlorine, bleach or acid which is accidentally mixed in food.

Cocktail party- An informal or semi- formal party at which alcoholic drinks are served.

Contract- A legal agreement between people, companies, etc.

Customer- Someone who buys goods or services from a business.

Cutlery- Spoons, forks and knives used for serving and eating.

Dessert- Sweet food eaten after the main part of the meal.

Dilute- To make something less strong by adding water or another liquid.

Enticing- To attract (someone) especially by offering or showing something that is appealing, interesting, etc.

Food hygiene- Also known as food safety, are the conditions and measures necessary to ensure the safety of food from production to consumption. Food can be contaminated at any point during slaughtering or harvesting, processing, storage, storage, distribution, transportation and preparation.

Food Poisoning- an acute gastrointestinal disorder caused by bacteria or their toxic products or by chemicals residues in food.

Food cost percentage- A number that is divided by your sales and a percentage of sales is calculated for the cost. So when you say you have a food cost of 40% that means you spent .40 for every peso you took in sales.

Function- An official or formal ceremony or social gathering

Guest- A customer at a hotel, restaurant or catering.

Hazard- A Source of danger.

Hygiene- Conditions or practices (as of cleanliness) conducive to health.

Insurance- Coverage by contract whereby one party undertakes to indemnify or guarantee another against loss by a specified risk or peril.

Main dish- is the featured or primary dish in a meal consisting of several courses.

Manpower- The total supply of persons available and fitted for service.

Menu- It is a list of food and beverage for sale in the food service establishment.

Napery- Table linen

Microorganism- an extremely small living things that can only be seen with a microscope.

Mushroom- A fungus that is shaped like an umbrella; especially: one that can be eaten.

Catering package- To put something together in order to sell it.

Customize- To change (something) in order to fit the needs or requirements of a person, business, etc.

Plated- A food that is served on a plate.

Pax- A term that refers to person or guest in the food service establishment.

Phraseology- The way that a particular person or group use words.

Physical Hazard- Are most recognized by consumers as they usually find this food safety hazard. Examples of physical hazards include: metal, glass, wood, insects, stones, soil, dirt, jewelry, hair, plasters and etc.

Salad- a mixture of raw green vegetables (such as different types of lettuce) usually combined with other raw vegetables.

Scale up- An increase according to a fixed ratio.

Side dish- A food served separately along with the main course.

Soup- A food made by cooking vegetables, meat, or fish in a large amount of liquid. The two kinds of soup are clear and think soup.

Toxin- A poisonous substance and especially one that is produced by a living thing.

INDEX